Might I Suggest

Might I Suggest

Becoming the One Clients Turn To,
Time and Time Again

Deb Feder

GRAMMAR
FACTORY
— EST? 2013 —

Published by Grammar Factory Publishing, an imprint of MacMillan Company Limited.
25 Telegram Mews, 39th Floor, Suite 3906
Toronto, Ontario, Canada M5V 3Z1
www.grammarfactory.com

Feder, Deb
Might I Suggest: Becoming the One Clients Turn To, Time and Time Again / Deb Feder.

Paperback ISBN 978-1-998528-70-7
Hardcover ISBN 978-1-998528-72-1
eBook ISBN 978-1-998528-71-4
Audiobook ISBN 978-1-998528-73-8

1. LAW056000 LAW / Law Office Management.
2. BUS020000 BUSINESS & ECONOMICS / Development / Business Development.
3. BUS058000 BUSINESS & ECONOMICS / Sales & Selling / General.

Production Credits
Cover design, book production and editorial services by Grammar Factory Publishing

*In deep appreciation for my parents
teaching me that our careers and lives never stop evolving.*

*For Andrew, who exemplifies
what it means to practice radical generosity.*

*And a quick reminder to my kids that
you can always bounce forward.*

Contents

We Begin

The very best first step to developing a book of business that brings incredible clients and opportunities to you over and over again is to decide to make it happen.

In January 2019, my business almost didn't exist. My revenue that month wouldn't cover our mortgage. What had been a healthy, thriving business shrank overnight as I juggled the impossible feat of managing my grandmother's health, running a business, and caring for a busy family. Turns out, my juggling skills weren't all that great. I had forgotten how I had built a career (and business), how to build balanced practices, and was living in crisis mode.

Now, the point of this story isn't the reality of the sandwich generation (although I have a lot to say about this) nor is it about financial communication (yeah, I have even more to say about that). It's about what came next...

One morning I found myself awake at 4 a.m., looking at my work and life and wondering what in the world had happened. It didn't take long for my muscle memory to kick in. I sent one email to family requesting support, and two additional emails to former colleagues and clients asking if they had time for lunch.

One morning and three connections changed everything.

That pivotal wake-up call at 4 a.m. wasn't an end to my business—it was a beginning.

Every time you close a transaction, finish a case, or handle a complex dispute, it feels more like an ending than a beginning. A client engagement ends, and it's time to worry about finding the next client. This transactional approach keeps you in a constant cycle of hunting for work and dreading every lull. The longer the lull, the more you fret.

When these moments arrive, you have four options:

1. **Overthink it.** Analyze every angle of every issue and gather all the options until mental exhaustion leaves you spent.

2. **Bury your head.** Become numb to the possibility of change and avoid thinking about it at all costs.

3. **Take the sub-par work that isn't all that exciting.** Rush to find anything that feels stable to avoid rocky feelings and potential financial impact.

4. **Take charge.** Proactively identify good choices by intentionally engaging with your network, spotting opportunities, and making grounded decisions.

As you might guess (since this is a book about building a self-sustaining practice through the strength of your network), I picked Option 4—and so should you.

The instinct to wait until after your latest deal or case closes is common. *Surely, you're much too busy to add anything to your plate; it's only logical to wait until you close out what you've got before figuring out what's next.* Yet the longer you wait, the longer the lull between work lasts, and the more likely you are to jump at the first opportunity that comes your way. It may resemble safety, but it's far from ideal.

Instead of waiting, opt in by raising your hand, doing something, and being present with your ideas and support.

The first step: rethink your approach to building a practice by treating it like a business you're responsible for. This makes you the CEO of your practice. When you understand your expertise and experience under this new lens, you can grow business from current clients and identify new ones that align with your goals, approach, and expertise. As you build relationships, people will trust and rely on you; in return, you can rely on them and the work that comes your way.

This model works whether you are running a business, growing a career, or managing a professional services practice. It starts with three key questions:

1. What does a strong business look like that doesn't require a continuous loop of hustling and hoping?
2. What do you have to do to make sure this happens?
3. How do you have to change to build a business that allows for a deep breath (at least every once in a while)?

These questions frame a business development model that isn't just successful, but sustainable.

Deconstructing How You Built Your Practice

Do you remember when you realized your role wasn't just to do the work? I do. As a new lawyer, I would wander the halls as soon as a project wrapped up, hoping someone would notice my slow walk by their door and jump out with an incredible project. After a lap or two with no prospects, I would settle back at my desk, cleaning up file folders and sending out a few notes to make sure I was on the radar of those who always had new projects coming. This was my "hope clients and colleagues think of me" phase. It's easy to feel stuck in this stage.

I remember the first time my role shifted. Months of doing the work and building relationships led to that first call. When that client asked if I would lead part of a team, I grabbed my notebook and checklist and marched into the project like my life depended on it. It wasn't the big step I thought it might be, but it was an important first step.

The lesson learned in that moment: That call—getting picked—happened because of the investment I'd made in the client and the work I had done for them.

Shifting my view of how to grow the practice I wanted (rather than following the path everyone said was "the way") changed everything. You can experience the same. Rather than fight the constraints of where you are now or what you feel is holding you back, learn to work with the natural and sometimes rocky growth of your practice. It's much easier and allows for much greater success.

Of course, it may not feel simple at first. Professional bumps are natural: some merely worrisome (slowing of work or hours not matching expectations); some more significant (when the one client you invested all your time in switches firms, closes a project, or changes strategy); others self-created (hurdles that arise from the desire to change and match market shifts and demands).

No matter the cause, thinking you can build a practice out of constant worry keeps you stuck. The fear might be that you'll never get work steady enough to build the expertise that sets you apart from the pack, or that this might be the last project you ever get. The stakes seem so high that any gap feels like it could be the end. This level of worry is enough to make anyone jumpy.

You barely pause to celebrate the project you just completed before the worry muscle kicks in and you start to crunch the numbers: hours billed, projects started, clients needed (broken down to the day) to hit your target by year's end. You agonize over your metrics, both for the near term and what's needed to get a head start on the new year.

If that doesn't exhaust you, it should. Yet this is what you're doing every time you assume your practice "isn't working" because work isn't showing up on your desk at a pace that feels steady and predictable.

See More by Shifting Your View

Instead of looking at what isn't working, focus on cultivating a thriving practice. One that is abundant in ideas, clients, and conversations. One that is challenging and fun. One that elevates you and your expertise to the point where the problems you're asked to solve and conversations you're asked to join energize you—a practice that prospers and flourishes without intense effort.

While the quest for a steady, stable practice seems like the goal, redefining it to be agile and flexible allows you to align your expertise, experience, energy, and enthusiasm to build not just a big book, but a quality practice you nurture each day. Even better is a practice that you are interested in (the subject matter) and invested in (the people).

This is the quest for a self-sustaining practice.

This book is about looking at your book of business, practice growth, and career from a different perspective. This happens when you focus on:

1. **Embracing evolution and growth** (versus fighting off all the "what ifs")

2. **Engaging in better conversations** (to identify opportunity, support, and ideas)

3. **Expanding your practice** by intentionally building a strong, healthy network (and cultivating those relationships)

4. **Choosing generosity** as a core value and practice that reaps exponential returns

You might be wondering why we're talking about your practice needing life support (or worse, your career falling apart) when this book is about the evolution of a professional practice. It's all a matter of perspective.

Consider how the lull plays out: Closing out one project requires being picked for another. Winning a case for a client means finding a new client with a case waiting for you. Growing your work to where you're asked to provide work for an entire team means you don't just need one client, but lots of them. The hunt for work, responsibility, clients, and business development is a constant loop of reboot-rethink-reimagine your priorities. This cycle demands that you constantly ask: "Now what?"[1]

These moments are not about falling apart—they're about growth.

This is not a story of failure. It's a story of evolution.

Some moments result from the changing world we live in; others happen because you're ready to change. Either way, learning what to do in this cycle allows you to control what happens next—versus crossing your fingers, hoping work remains steady, clients remember you, and the hard work that got you here will be enough.

Instead of thinking *oh shit!* and readying yourself for a panic attack, reframe these moments as pivot points. Better yet, growth. Because when you're in client relationships that recognize your value and you allow yourself to share it, the role you're known for changes. You are no longer just a recipient of tasks or a mere helper; you're an advisor... a strategist... a key member of the team.

This allows calm in the center of these pivotal moments. As the person clients turn to when their business is evolving, your practice grows and evolves in response. This is the business model and entrepreneurial mindset that a quality practice employs.

---

1 This approach also works when your practice needs to move organizations, or when you launch a practice within an organization or on your own. If you want to build a career for the long haul in the ever-changing environment and institutional priorities of private practice, you'll need this skill in your back pocket.

Own Your Growth

My January 2019 story could have easily ended with getting a couple new clients, taking a deep breath, and juggling family obligations with grace. This isn't a made-for-television movie. Instead, it forced me to look at my business and the strategies I used with clients from a whole new angle. The goal is to make sure the practice thrives when life happens, not if it happens. Because it happens to us all.

Taking a more holistic (and dare I say, healthy) approach asks you to understand the scope of your strengths: what you need to learn about your business and your clients' business, the relationships you have, and how expanding your network opens you up to new possibilities and prospects.

This change in focus takes all you've learned through years of practicing and positions you for what's next. This growth might be something you're looking for or forced into, but it's always a reimagining of your practice to align with a new stage of maturity and opportunity.

The fact is, all mature careers evolve over time due to a variety of factors (many of which are discussed in this book). A self-sustaining practice isn't something that happens from the beginning and continues on autopilot. It requires proactive and continual rethinking and reimagining of potential and possibilities. It isn't a solo effort (although self-reflection is part of it), but it's most beneficial when you, your clients, colleagues, and communities are part of it. When done right, it's reciprocal. It allows you to participate in their work such that they trust you to show up and help them think through their important questions.

- A self-sustaining practice brings work to you because of what you do and who you are.

- A self-sustaining practice is scalable to embrace the commitments you have to yourself and your team.

- A self-sustaining practice keeps work rolling your way.

When you decide you're ready to shift your practice from one that's simply there when someone needs you to one that allows you to connect, nurture, and grow relationships, it changes everything. It's how you shift from doing what you've always done, to growing the practice you've dreamed of—resulting in meaningful work that energizes you.

A Side Note About Regret

"How do you shake the feeling that you wish you had done things differently?" It's a question I get asked a lot. While I want you to understand how you got here, this isn't a lecture on how you could have experienced a different outcome.

The powerful pull of hindsight makes you believe you would've done something different with better information. Yet most decisions that brought you to this point were based on the best information you had at the moment and the priorities that were most critical at that time. You can't hit the reset button, but you can find the gifts in the knowledge and expertise you honed, the people you met, and the things you learned about yourself and others along the way. This gives grace for the path that got you here. It also allows you to recognize that career growth isn't just an accumulation of knowledge but also includes a combination of your relationships, conversations, and mindset.

The art of transforming professional regret into rocket fuel for your next chapter deserves its own deeper exploration, but that's a conversation for another time…

Building a Mature Practice

Let's clear up a few misconceptions about growing a professional practice. No matter what it looks like from the outside when you see that super successful colleague down the hall, I can assure you (since I've talked to many of them) it wasn't all smooth sailing on a consistent upward trajectory that created that success.

Remember:

- A practice isn't built once and never revisited in scope or structure.

- A practice doesn't grow just by managing the work on your desk.

- A practice rarely grows by huge leaps overnight.

Using hindsight as the guide, the growth and expansion of a practice often happen in micro-moments you experience at the end of each project, case, or opportunity.[2]

---

2   It even happens when you hang up the phone from an unexpected conversation that changes everything. Yeah, more on that later…

The natural reimagining of your network, conversations, and expertise is not evidence that you have failed. In fact, this reimagining allows you to make intentional choices that are personal and appropriate for you and your practice's growth. It's not evidence that you haven't made it or that you're behind. Rather, the simple acknowledgment and decision to make it part of your practice is your success story in the making.

There's a secret within this quest that might as well come out upfront. You aren't hunting for the pinnacle destination of a practice. You aren't building your business up to its peak. You are redefining the evolution of your practice and embracing what clients need most right now. By showing up for the "right now" moments, your role as a trusted advisor goes beyond the latest singular project and becomes part of a greater client relationship. This is where the fun begins.

Clients want and need help making good decisions. Having someone they know and trust as part of their "team" allows them to rely on you and your advice. In a world filled with explosive technologies, successful practitioners understand the role that a strategic thinking partner holds in helping clients make better decisions.

Before building a practice that cultivates clients, your career is stuck in its adolescent phase. As it grows and matures, you move beyond calculating billable hours and originations on repeat and start contemplating new business conversations and the client relationships that might result from sharing your expertise. Showing up for clients in the micro-conversations that happen every day is the cornerstone of a steady practice. The compensation and respect speak for themselves. You're no longer hoping to be noticed in a crowded field of semi-experts professing to be the one to know. Clients come to you because you simply are the one to know.

Clients are desperate for those willing and able to show up at this level of thought and care. There's no need to beg for attention, because there's true depth of understanding and investment in the personal and professional relationships that emerge from advisory roles.

This book shows you how it's done.

It takes your everyday conversations and interactions and layers them with modern strategy for building quality relationships that evolve as the clients, you, and your career need them to. Clients are ready for your opinions and advice—when they are informed by a deeper understanding, not only of your expertise, but also of their business and goals.

My work to this point has focused on getting into conversations (as I spell out in *After Hello*) and expanding those conversations to build trusted client relationships (which we work through in *Tell Me More*). What you do with these foundational skills will determine what happens after you offer up, *Might I Suggest...*

Each of these key conversation strategies is built with versatility and efficiency in mind. *Hello* opens the door and allows you to engage in conversation, build a network, and introduce yourself. *Tell Me More* puts you in the position to actively engage in building your everyday relationships by listening and learning. *Might I Suggest* asks that you step up as the advisor and not just listen but participate. When the client gives you the nod, it instantly changes the trajectory of the conversation. Once the client responds with "Sure, I'm listening," there's an opening and a whole new focus.

Allow Your Advisory Role to Evolve

Building a modern professional practice requires you to consider not only the skills and knowledge necessary to stay relevant but also to reimagine the advisory role in its entirety. Thanks to technological advances and the scope of knowledge available at anyone's fingertips, the role of trusted thinking partner and outside advisor has shifted (and will continue to shift) from being someone who can find the answer to someone whose judgment in thinking through the decisions is of far greater value.

Once you own your role in this professional business model, you can rethink the advice you give and who relies on that advice. You begin to think of each client interaction in terms of reliability. You go beyond the simple metric of a billable hour to deepen your relationships such that the generosity of your knowledge and ideas is not only welcome but expected.[3] You engage with clients such that you understand the complexities of a situation often discovered in the midst of simple conversations.

You can wait for the wake-up call to own your practice like I did in 2019, or commit now to treating your career like

---

3   Just like clients know what they are getting when they walk into their favorite store, they should experience the same when they pick up the phone to talk to you. Some call this branding (or otherwise try to make it fancy). For right now, let's consider it being reliable and consistent in putting yourself out there and showcasing your work, approach, and personality with clients.

a business, with you as the CEO. It will make the growth strategy easier to identify and help ensure your efforts align with the outcomes you wish to generate. The pages of this book lay out the habits that support the shifts in mindset and vision that are required. More importantly, you'll learn the habits and daily choices that naturally cultivate a practice that generates opportunity, over and over again. With that, let's get started.

Your Task List[4]

1. **Think of your practice as a self-sustaining business.** This requires you to have a monthly business meeting where you consider better metrics, which we'll call your Monthly Meeting.[5] As the business side of your practice, you need to report back to yourself on what's working, what's not, and where you are in terms of spotting, and regularly following up with, prospects. Consider this meeting non-negotiable.

2. **Create an agenda template for this meeting.** Keep the agenda simple and flexible. Close each Monthly Meeting with action steps and a dance party to celebrate a great meeting.

3. **Pick one project or client that, if you could wave a magic wand, you would put on repeat.** The client energizes you, the conversations are good, and the work is interesting. It doesn't feel like drudgery. Not only that, but it's fun. Brainstorm what you love about it. What makes the project interesting? What makes working with that client enjoyable? Describe with as much detail as possible.[6]

---

4 Throughout the book, please note Your Task List. These simple to-dos take the theories and examples discussed and allow you to put them into practice—not just once but on a routine basis for your practice strategy. You can take these tasks one step further with the *Might I Suggest* resources found at https://debfeder.com/clients.

5 Notice that I suggest this be a monthly meeting—not more frequent. Too often, I find clients obsessing over metrics like dollars in, dollars out, originations, and hours. But just because you billed 6.7 hours on this day in June of last year but only billed 5.2 hours on the same day this year doesn't mean you're behind. It's time to widen your view.

6 The mistake here is thinking that you should only go after this kind of work. Instead, I want you to focus on being aware of what works, what clients are aligned, and where they are showing up (or not) in your big stack of work. Being aware is the first step in growing the practice you want.

Get a Clear View of How You Work

If you always look at your practice and what you want to grow the same way, it's difficult to cultivate work or client relationships in any new way.

Living in Iowa City one summer, a particularly brutal storm blew through town, leaving me huddled in the basement of a tiny student house all by myself. There were no smartphones. I had to stretch the long cord of the kitchen wall phone to talk to my parents, out of my mind with worry, watching the storm break the house windows and start to flood the basement while I pondered the best options for myself and the dog I was housesitting. After the storm blew through, I headed to the store and bought the biggest flashlight I could find. That flashlight wasn't just huge; it had an incredible number of settings. One setting could light up the whole house, while another cast a very bright light over a distance, perfect for walks. Not only was I no longer scared of the dark street that had lost power, but I also felt in control and ready to conquer whatever the world (and Mother Nature) tossed my way.

There is something that happens when you shine that kind of light on the path before you. Suddenly, the blemishes and cracks come into focus. The way forward becomes apparent, as what you could not see in the dark becomes more and more visible.

Forgive the analogies tied to my badass flashlight, but as you will see in the coming pages, what you look at and the lens through which you focus matter.

Again, much like me and that flashlight, part of building a self-sustaining practice is finding a way to tap into this inner hero who knows how to conquer whatever comes your way while keeping a practice afloat.[7] It may be the client crisis or momentary, non-existent workload. It may also be the complexities of finding that next client, getting a new client onboarded, the work launched, or the issues resolved. (Speaking of which, issues arrive even as—or because— clients become more comfortable with you and the team.) In other words, it's always something. Knowing how to coexist with each of these challenges and still love what you do is the superpower to focus on here.

The Mindset Shift

Heroes don't just stand up and proclaim their greatness. They don't shine the light on themselves, as it were, but they know where to focus their attention and what to lead others to see. (In the interest of full disclosure, I will try to tone down the cheesy light metaphors, but they do help frame what's next.)

In a law practice, your focus shows up in how you spend your days and who gets your attention. You need to shift the view from trying to get everything done to aligning your

---

7   Those who know me know I constantly talk about building, managing, growing, and expanding a practice all at the same time. It starts right here. You have to step away from thinking management gets all the attention and know how to handle the growth and challenges all at the same time.

choices and daily actions in a way that grows the work and moves you one step closer to a mature practice.

In addition, reaching your personal best isn't just a proclamation that you are going to rise to the ranks of leadership and industry and assume it will work out (or step on everyone in your wake until it does). It certainly doesn't happen by hoping for the opportunity and waiting for others to follow your lead. Your personal best starts by knowing you, where you are right now, and where you need to focus on maturing next. Taking this sort of personal inventory and identifying these growth points require reflection. You need to understand where you are in building your expertise, managing your days, growing your practice, and rising when the opportunity presents itself to expand your influence. You do this by simply pausing and asking yourself: when you invest in your practice, where do you spend your time and mental energy?

1. Are you spending all your time trying to get up to speed on the knowledge necessary for your practice, or explaining it to others? (This is building.)

2. Are you spending all your time just trying to make sure you are doing the work, keeping track of the work, and organizing the work? (This is managing.)

3. Do you spend more time trying to secure that next project from a client or colleague, or work a bit smarter to get more out of each day? (This is growing.)

4. Are your big ideas and energy focused on the clients and opportunities that could have exponential growth? (This is expanding.)

Spend some time thinking about each of these questions and identify ways you give each energy. Do you notice which questions get more of your time and energy? This simple acknowledgement also allows you to see where to shift your attention to ensure balanced practice growth. Understanding these patterns will help you set clear intentions and achieve better results moving forward.

Balancing these four areas allows you to not just work at your personal best but find easy entries to growth. The real challenge comes when you then pause and ask how this influences the rest of your time, energy, self-care, and commitments. Personal best does not mean leaving any part of your life behind; it means finding a way to make sure all parts work together. When aligned in your approach, integrating work with your life becomes much easier.

Stop Doing Everything

When your view is only on the billable hour metric, it's easy to focus on filling that bucket up day after day with whatever comes your way, making sure you never feel behind in doing what you think you're supposed to be doing. This never-ending pursuit of meeting that big year-end goal can fill your practice until you're functioning solely in chase-mode. And the chase often forgets to make sure the work you have is what you want.

How do you get out of this cycle? It starts by giving some of it away. As work comes in, there is an essential first question that must be asked: "Who else can do this work?" When you start with this inquiry, you build a habit of rejecting the assertion that you are supposed to know everything and do everything.

Now, I can almost hear you grumbling in the pages of this book: *It's easier to do the work myself... it takes too long to train... the work won't be done right... I don't have the team to rely on... my clients won't trust me if I have others working on their work... I need the hours so I might as well do it.* A mature practice relaxes the hyper-focus on these worries and builds a better team by delegating and sharing the workload.

Allowing your team to do the work that is not the best use of your time and expertise does three things:

1. Opens up your day for more important work that is waiting for you and needs your level of expertise and attention.

2. Opens up space for you to focus on work and clients that fill your bucket (or, dare I say, on work you find interesting and enjoyable) and is sustainable.

3. Invests in the careers of others because they can now do what you do and start creating their own self-sustaining practice.

It's simple: if you never allow others to step in and learn the work and how to work with clients, you will always have to be the one doing it all, which will leave little to no time to do anything else. This loop creates the self-fulfilling prophecy of working yourself into a business development hole.

- The client might shift strategies and no longer need you. *Oops, you are out of work.*

- The work might become obsolete with the change in regulations or statutory landscape. *Oops, you are out of work.*

- A new technology shifts the protocols or requirements for the limited scope of work you do. *Oops, you are out of work.*

- The client might retire, and the new team has their own team. *Oops, you are out of work.*

You get the point. Since you are doing all the work, the billable work dries up, and the client development starts back at zero. In this scenario, it's not about putting all your eggs in one basket, it's that you aren't allowing your basket to be big enough to fit others. The old approach doesn't allow room to diversify your attention to clients and identify and capitalize on what's next.

Instead, let others do work they are capable of and train those ready to step up in their own practices. Create a system where others are working with you. Let them depend on you and your work.

To get that faucet of client development flowing a bit stronger and keep new work heading your way, ask yourself these questions:

1. Who else can jump in and help me out with this work?

2. To stop chasing updates from my team, who can send me project updates each week and take responsibility for the project tracking?

3. What other steps do I need to put into place to get comfortable with letting delegation be a cornerstone of my practice?

Getting stuff off your desk allows you to rethink how you prioritize your days, starting from what happens the moment you first sit down at your desk each day.[8]

---

8 How do you make sure your team has an approach that replicates the way you built up trust with the client to expand this work? Communication and training. Yeah, I love to talk about that too—more to come soon.

Two Hoots

Another key shift as the CEO of your work and world is decid-
ing what you care about (or have the capacity to care about).
My rule is simple: on any given day, you have the capacity
to give two hoots, not ten.[9] Narrowing down your priorities
to what is truly important is critical to understanding what
gets your attention and where you need to find the energy
and focus.

If business development is critical to your annual goals, but it
is never given the attention until your practice is at a tipping
point, then it will never gain the traction you are seeking. If
you keep focusing on office politics, then your energy will be
diverted in ways that leave you little time to focus on the stuff
that can positively impact your work, clients, and daily life.
While the distractions and priorities of others won't necessarily disappear, you can help them fade into the distance by
picking out your two priorities (or hoots) each day.

Rather than picking the two most obvious priorities, cultivate
a habit that allows you to align this daily choice of cares from
an energetic and holistic look at your life. If your kids are
going through a big transition or challenging spot, then they
may get one of your hoots. If your health needs your attention,
give it the hoot. If a client has a transaction that needs your
full attention, one hoot. You get the point. By starting with
the critical question, you can identify where to place your
hoots. If you have one remaining, consider what is necessary
for your practice to develop in alignment with where you
want it to grow, rather than what seems like the hot crisis on
your plate. Make sure your business priorities are reflected in
your cares.

---

9   You can replace "hoots" with whatever term you want. You really just get two significant cares in a day.

Staying Busy isn't Really a Strategy

When you are in the thick of doing the work on your desk, it's often a routine and rhythm on repeat: get up, check email, do the work, handle the issues that feel like fire drills, check in on the deadlines, answer the calls, do the work, handle the fires. Over and over again. Inserting business development and practice growth into this routine doesn't work unless you rethink how your days and time can look. Notice this isn't about magically finding hours, but the mindset of your time and what gets your attention. This requires you to break up the days in a way that shifts your view.

Clients frequently send me notes asking for time management solutions—preferably an app that will just take care of everything for them. What I have found is that the most reliable solution must work with and for the life of a professional service provider. Billing in six-minute cycles that are constantly interrupted requires you to stay aware and engaged with the phone and inbox throughout the day so you can deal with unexpected fires but also maintain the level of client availability needed to "do the job."

Now, this will not become a treatise or an opinion on availability, but the following approach blends it all.

- **Step One:** Pick your two priorities the night before.[10]

- **Step Two:** Start your day with one of those priorities, preferably a thirty-minute billable or client-focused task. This will launch your day with .5 in billable time.[11]

---

10 I remember reading *The 4-Hour Workweek* and considering how Tim Ferriss focuses on two priorities each day, but the approach here takes into account the need for billable hours and getting some traction on getting the "stuff to do" done.

11 I get asked about the Pomodoro Technique frequently. It starts with a twenty-five-minute time block, but I find thirty minutes works better for those billing time and keeps the morning routine balanced with quick tasks.

- **Step Three:** Set a timer for five minutes and triage your inbox. More on this later, but this is not the time to answer emails. Pretend you're on *Grey's Anatomy* and need to prioritize patients: find the emergencies, file and delete what you can, and sideline the rest.

- **Step Four:** Set a timer for five more minutes. Send one email (or make a call or send a text) to nurture your network.

- **Step Five:** Take a five-minute break. This is a great time to get a drink of water, say *Hello* to a colleague, or stretch.

When you come back from your break, consider: Do you need to focus on important emails or prep for a call with a potential client? Can you conquer that second billable task or do you need to finish the first? Blending productivity (getting something done) with purpose (building a practice that is sustaining, rather than chasing your work like it's on life support) is not only a new perspective but a dramatic shift in energy with which to approach the growth of your practice.

This forty-five-minute routine starts your day off with a bang.[12]

Billable work—check! Inbox—check! Business Development —check!

If nothing else happens in your day, if it ends up being a client fire drill day, you've still been thoughtful about moving a bigger billable priority forward. And you completed something that nurtures and engages your network for the purpose of building your book. When you put this habit in motion, your view

---

12   OK. It really starts your day off with a good blend of productivity, business development, and organization. This is kind of like an amazing cup of coffee for your practice.

changes; you've done so much in less time than it normally takes you to start answering emails and figuring out your day. The goal is to see what's in front of you differently.

Who Gets Your Attention

In the routine of work, it's easy to see how some clients get more of your attention than others. There are those who raise their voices in moments of stress, others simply have a volume of work that continues to raise them up in your inbox. These clients are visible.

The next layer of clients is significant. They bring you a bigger project, a more substantial case, something that requires a bigger chunk of your time and attention.

But both the visible and significant assume that you are paying attention to the clients and matters that are the loudest, most urgent on your desk at any given moment. You aren't strategically looking at the client relationships to nurture, you're simply engaging with the ones who need you right now.

The self-sustaining practice pushes you out of this cycle by shifting your view from focusing on the loud and omnipresent to evening out your attention to include evolving relationships.

For this section, gather your network notes. If you're unfamiliar, I often refer to a simple Networking Nurture List that tracks the relationships you are currently nurturing. This isn't your whole contact list, but a simple spreadsheet that was introduced in

Tell Me More.[13] Now is the time to dive into your network to consider which clients and relationships are getting your attention right now, and who is waiting for you to engage.

First, looking back at the last month, notice who you talked to. Who did you speak to most frequently? Were there others who you intended to connect with but never seemed to have time to make the call? The people you're putting off just might be the most important people in the coming months. The longer you wait, the greater the chance that this relationship will need more of a reboot than a touch-base in the coming months.

Notice how often you connect with anyone other than active clients. If you are only communicating with the active work, you are stuck in the cycle of managing and doing the work. You need to strategically add interesting and engaging conversations into your month that cultivate a broader reach of relationships and workflow. The goal is to create a workflow that generates in the background while you are busy doing the work you've got right now.[14]

Next, notice how energized you feel by the conversations you are having in the present. If you don't love the work and direction of your practice, it's most often a result of where you give your energy and focus. Shift your view by using that flashlight view and recognize where you give your attention. Maybe find a set of binoculars and look around

---

13 Join me at https://debfeder.com/clients to learn more and get your Networking Nurture List set up.

14 The same type of reflection is necessary for those working within companies. If you're only talking to the teams that need your input right now, you are simply hoping all the others will think to loop you in when ready. Stay ahead of the game by proactively building broader relationships.

your practice for a new view of what other people are doing and who they are talking to. Yeah, this feels like spying, but in this case, it is not just appropriate but useful.

One more view to consider: if there were no limitations, who would you want to be talking to and engaging with? Take some notes, as these are good guides to where your attention needs to shift and the connections worth nurturing going forward.[15]

A Wider View of Your Practice

There is more to be found by looking around. This intentional widening of your view forces you to not just think about what work lies ahead but describe it in excruciating detail. Simply wanting to grow (without direction) is a hazardous growth plan. It often leads to unexpected complications with needy clients, playing it small, or taking care of the leftovers—projects that those with clearer direction know aren't meant for them. To both build and manage your practice effectively, you need to ensure your time isn't slipping away to the wrong priorities. If it is, that's an obstacle you need to tackle to give your growth the space and oxygen to expand.

Consider:

- **Industry shifts:** These are not just driven by online hype or the impact of AI (although both are important) but also trends you spot from the years that built your expertise. Before long, you'll start to predict changes that will define your practice, clients, and industry.

---

15 It is possible here that you don't know the people you wish you were talking to, or have a tenuous, at best, social media connection with them. Still, write them down and we can tackle the next step that helps you navigate that conversation without feeling creepy.

- **Hidden opportunities:** Looking ahead gives you the unique insight to spot what others might overlook or not even recognize as opportunities.

- **New players:** As you see a more complete picture, you can start recognizing the influential people and players within the industry who not only need to be on your radar, but also part of your network.

- **Your own personal growth:** Life hands you a variety of lessons and moments that change who you are as a human and what you want and expect for yourself. The natural desire to keep learning and growing pushes at a practice that has gone stagnant; it often demands that you shift into the next stage, because everything feels like it doesn't quite fit anymore.[16]

This quick gathering of intel on your networking strategy and current conversations allows you to shift the view to a forward-thinking approach that doesn't just find work but helps you create the new cycle of nurturing relationships and your network, knowing where your expertise is wanted to help work come your way.

Case Study: A Better View Allows You to Give Better Advice

An example of this comes from my client, Anna. Anna is a fierce competitive athlete who is often found embracing a self-directed physical goal that finds her climbing (literally and figuratively) to new heights. Her clients' goals often mirror competitive physical goals, which requires knowing which priority needs attention at a given time. Anna brings a unique empathy and understanding to her clients and their goals.

---

16 There is so much more to say about this and we'll get to it soon. For now, it's important to recognize that as your practice evolves, so will you.

Now, Anna takes a wide-angle view of her work and how it supports the whole life of her clients. She doesn't just bring a wealth of experience to the table, but years of working as a corporate executive and as a parent to two teens who have taught her the value of understanding the whole picture. Anna understands how to focus on the important and balance it with the patience needed to guide clients to solutions that work for them. This wide view allows her to give better advice and continue growing a healthy book of business. Anna's advisory role is that much better because she doesn't just try to make sure her clients value her; she focuses on blending the right advice needed from her clients' perspective.

How Well Do You Know Your Clients

While getting a clear view of your practice is important, it's equally important to have this same clarity about your clients. In *Tell Me More*, I laid out the framework for asking better questions. By asking better questions, you allow client relationships to deepen through your genuine ability to let curiosity find the layers of a client's issues and business they're ready to share with you. But to give good, if not (dare I say) great advice, you need to take this a step further. You need to understand their business and industry priorities, challenges, and frameworks from a whole new perspective.

Consider these questions as you move forward:

- Who do your clients consider their target audience?

- How well can you describe their ideal clients?

- What are the three most important priorities your clients have right now?

- What would you like to know if you could have one hour in conversation with a client without any interruptions?

If your answer to this final question is how to get hired, it's time to learn more. Start by downloading the guide: *Know Your Clients*.[17] This tool will not only help you gain clarity but also know what to do with this information once it's collected.

***

Chances are good you have a decent idea about where you want your practice to go (seeing how you picked up this book on a self-sustaining practice and all). But if you don't have a clear view of how you currently work and what it's creating, you're basically moving about in the dark. You need to take a good honest look at the path to ensure you are equipped to navigate the bumps along the way and turn them into growth points.

---

17 Download *Know Your Clients* at https://debfeder.com/clients and get started fine-tuning a key component of building your practice like you would run a business.

Your Task List

1. **Pick one client and look closely at how your relationship evolved and the types of projects they bring to you.** How has the work evolved over time? When was the last time you sat down and strategized with this client over what's next for them? No need to do anything right now other than take a closer look and make some notes.

2. **Remember the two-hoot strategy?** Instead of jumping into the strategy, take one week to reflect at the end of each day on what your two hoots were and whether they distracted or served your practice goals and business growth. This will serve as a starting metric to shift your choices going forward.

3. **Practice sharing your expertise and ideas with a client or colleague by talking through an update to the work you do together.** Map out what you want to share before you go into the conversation, paying specific attention to the action steps you want others to consider from talking with you.

Be Steady,
Not Shiny

*Be open to finding the cornerstone of your
practice that interests and attracts clients
(over and over again).*

In 1981, my parents' business hit a tipping point. Interest rates approached twenty percent and the resulting
construction cost projections could make anyone puke,
making their construction-management business model
beg for an instant makeover. Until that point, their business had been a whole family affair of building and
managing apartment buildings in Cedar Rapids, Iowa.
When my parents went searching for a second business to
diversify, their primary focus was finding one with a solid
foundation. Refusing to be stuck in economic reactive
mode, they anchored their decision with one fundamen-
tal question: what will people always need? Knowing
whatever they picked had a laundry list of inherent risks,
they landed on food through the assumption that people would always need to eat. This entrepreneurial spirit
wasn't chasing the hot new thing, but the solid, needed

commodity that could create some stability for their business, financial, and life goals.[18]

Now, this makes sense from a company perspective, but how does this apply to the professional services industry? It is the exact same model. You need a base for your practice, and then the ability to continuously guide it through the evolution, reinvention, and reboots that are the natural cycle of any career with longevity.

Before you create a new steadiness in your practice, let's clarify what this is not. It often feels safe to focus on a book of business with clients and projects that are repeatable and dependable. But "safe" is a misnomer, because it discounts the one thing that is certain to happen: change. Practices, technology, laws, people, and priorities constantly shift. Assuming you can build a thriving book from doing the same work over and over again and filling your plate "just enough" doesn't create the strong book you are looking for. In fact, it often leads to a different inflection point in this series. It creates boredom, which leads to a desire to reimagine what you do and to seek out new challenges that use the skills you have built from repeatable work. Instead of chasing what's safe, focus on rethinking what clients can steadily count on from you.

---

18 You may wonder how I know and remember all this from forty-plus years ago. My mom used to drop career and life advice on us while driving carpool. It sounded something like this: "Hey, I know you are headed to ballet, but when you sell a business make sure to get three appraisals," or "Remember to make sure your career can withstand the economy." It would be sprinkled right along with a plan for dinner, family vacation, and an argument about who got the front seat. While my siblings and I don't always agree on the dinner plans, we all remember the discussions about life and business planning.

Let Clients Count on You

Clients appreciate reliability. They want an advisor who is consistent in approach and availability and has equally invested the time and energy to know them (as humans) but also to really understand their business. This doesn't happen by showing up, but by actively learning. Setting news alerts to stay abreast of changes is one level. But really understanding the business, operations, and industry landscape takes your advice and relationships from being the one to call for the important legal project to being the one that can be counted on to provide wise counsel from a more comprehensive view.[19] The topics and needs might not always be the most interesting, but having a solid foundation in your practice and knowledge of the industries you support allows you to build a much steadier book of business. It also allows you to grow into the incredible client relationships you've always dreamed of managing.

Notice the shift here. The focus is not being the one to know (getting your expertise seen and heard) but learning about others. This changes everything. Here are a few ways you can put this into action by staying open and curious about others:

1. **In a conversation, ask what they are up to these days.** This wide-open question allows the client to vent and share all they are working on, worried about, and spending all their time on.

---

19 Notice the use of different tools here that give you a better view to make stronger choices. By getting closer to understanding the business model (magnifying glass), you gain a wider view (binoculars). In turn, you can help the client navigate what no one sees coming and the foundation of the business (flashlight).

2. **Read the company's news alerts.** Don't just read the headlines, but dive into the company's news releases, public relations statements, and what the media has to say. Get as many angles as you can. Start to put yourself in your client's shoes.

3. **Answer the small questions without ever thinking about writing down your time.**

Now, take a deep breath. I know the third item in that list makes you worry that I'm suggesting that you just keep giving away time and never get to put your billable investment on paper. That is not the case. This is not the time to panic, but to calmly consider what you ultimately want from the client:

- To call you with the questions

- To pick you for the big projects

- To see you at the industry gatherings and know you are there and in the know (to provide introductions and insight)

- To rely on your wisdom to the point where you're not just on their legal team, but helping them set legal budgets, priorities, and strategy

If you hurry them into a billable moment every time you talk about anything and everything, including answering the random quick question, they will think you simply want to remain a transactional resource. It speaks to your work style and priorities. You have to set down the chase for the incremental billable hour and consider the investment in the relationship by engaging in conversations. All the time.

Instead of trying to upsell clients and sound impressive with your knowledge in every call, show up human and engaged in the work. This allows you to get to the meat of the work a whole lot faster and gets more billable work sent your way. In fact, it often works best to show clients how you can save them time, money, or trouble. If the client can sleep better at night because of your strategy, it's a home run.[20]

Narrowing down your expertise and being able to describe the foundation of your work is important. But the expectation that clients can count on you matters even more. It transcends any actual legal need and is a signpost of a mature practice—one that can be noticed up close and at a distance. It is also what sets you apart from competitors and builds your reputation. How you deliver the work is in essence your practice style.

Show Up for the Client Relationship

When you look at all the things you wonder and worry about in a day, they often fall into buckets of what you can control and influence, and what you cannot. Instead of trying to change others or hope for someone to think of you, simply look in the mirror. The one thing you can control is yourself and how you show up for others.

The research around human dynamics, problem solving, and workplace satisfaction continues to point to the need to interact directly with our colleagues and clients.[21] This means finding a strategy that keeps you in the mix of these

---

20 Be the client's trusted advisor and thinking partner. It is the coveted spot that far too many are walking by, assuming that it requires a formal invitation.

21 Check out this article from the *Harvard Business Review* about what makes our work meaningful (https://hbr.org/2023/07/what-makes-work-meaningful).

discussions and allows your practice to grow to the level of being involved in the more complex, dynamic, strategic decisions.

While ever-evolving technologies may support all of this, the key is knowing which technology helps you be more intentional and personal in your strategy. Because communicating complex legal or accounting methods is one thing, but understanding how to show up for clients in a way that nurtures, grows, and expands your practice is a different type of connection.

What does it mean to show up for clients? Typically, it means you are known to be two things: responsive and approachable. Interestingly, these mean different things to different people. For some, it means clients are comfortable bringing their ideas and questions to you. For others, it means you're available for off-the-wall questions and ideas. For others still, it means you are welcoming in your availability—you don't put on airs, put up guardrails, or otherwise make clients feel you can't be bothered.

Regardless of meaning, professional service advisors are the helpline clients and companies need to get stuff off their plate and get better advice than what is available to them within their own organization. With this in mind, you need to show up not just for the big project and bigger deadlines, but for the daily interactions and conversations.

Here's what this looks like in a practical sense:

- When someone reaches out with a question, find time to talk or let them know you are on it. They just want to know you've got it and will get back to them.

- When a client or prospective client has an idea, show up willing to brainstorm or make connections that seem aligned with the bigger picture strategy in question.

- When someone calls you, make sure they aren't building a relationship with your voicemail.

- When you forget to follow up, circle back and let them know it's still on your radar.

Now that clients know you are "on it", you need to make sure your work is delivered in a way that separates you from the pack. This means using all the work you've done to provide good, clear answers to clients. It gets better by asking questions that not only inform the work product they are asking for but allow you to discover and deliver the depth of advice they are looking for. It also allows clients to refer others to you based on knowing you are the one to know.

There is a richness in your practice that evolves when you decide to level up your expertise and approach. It is a whole lot more fun when clients not only rely on you, but when the questions they ask light you up. This happens by spending time learning, staying current with trends, and practicing the explanations to the point where you know the exact language that will resonate with clients. It happens inside the conversation with clients rather than from the sidelines. It happens when you pick up the phone. Being open and available cannot be dismissed in this equation.

Be an Opportunity Creator

The key to a successful, self-sustaining practice is one in which there isn't just work to be done, but great work—work that energizes you, aligns with your priorities and goals (yeah, this includes billable hours and rates), and gives you options.

When thinking about options, I am always drawn to the analogy from a good friend of mine who eloquently explained how he talked to his kids about life opportunities. He explained that your goal is to keep as many options as possible available to you and consider whether a choice might limit (or even eliminate) opportunities going forward.

Enter the Big Sticky Note Wall

I highly encourage you at this point to grab a pack of sticky notes and put blank ones all over a wall. Consider these options and opportunities. What you do and how you cultivate your practice decides whether more sticky notes are added to the wall, or whether some end up in the garbage. Talking to clients and being consistent with your networking strategy (see Chapters 9 and 10) adds options. Skipping every client meeting removes some. Not interested in the partners talking through a client strategy that doesn't seem to apply to you (remove a sticky), pausing and learning more (add one). You get the point.

The goal is not to be doing all the work of all the clients represented by all the sticky notes, but to have choices.

These choices aren't just hallmarks of a strong career, but one that sustains itself and provides agency over the direction and depth of your work.

Predictability in your practice deepens significantly with consistent engagement with your network. The people behind your work and in your sphere are the foundation of steadiness. Their knowledge of you, and your priorities, expertise, and goals shift what you are trying to build from simply being your problem to something others can support and promote with you. While the relationship building strategy will go a long way in moving you on the right path, paying attention to the mindset and care you bring to your network and relationships acts like a glue stick in making the results so much better. Creating a stickiness between yourself and your network happens in the energy and attitude that you show up with and allow others to engage with.

The best part: when you start to embrace the sticky note choices, you are no longer pointing fingers at what others are doing to your practice. You can see your own role in how it unfolds. You can also change it quickly.

***

From this point forward, your network and how you choose to engage with it defines the work style you design and what others can count on from you. From a business perspective, your clients need to rely on your practice, which means not only being steady but allowing others to see and experience all that you do.

Your Task List

1. **Consider your dream client.** What are their expectations for you as the professional they want to hire? What should their expectations be? How might this change in five to ten years and how will that change the way they count on you?

2. **Take charge of your workdays.** This is critical to being the owner of your practice. How have you designed them to show up for clients? Does this approach work for you? What tweaks could you make that would allow your days and availability to work better for yourself and your clients? Find the win-win ideas and make a list. Don't try to shift all at once. Instead, consider one small change that might open up a different way to be the steady support clients need, without adding undue chaos to your days.

3. **Review the snapshot of your knowledge gaps from earlier in the chapter.** Write yourself a letter five years from now describing your practice and days. This doesn't need to be a novel, just a simple note about the incredible ways your career, practice, and expertise have evolved. Tuck it away to look at later.

Radiate Infectious Energy

Find the joy in what you love about what
you do and then sprinkle that like confetti
in your conversations. It's contagious.

When I was in law school, my friends decided that spring break called for a trip to the mountains. Not wanting to be left out of the fun, I not only agreed to join the trip but volunteered to be a driver on the overnight ride across Nebraska. The trip had *bad idea* written all over it from the beginning. First, I have a strong dislike for road trips (hence the volunteering to drive—at least I was in the front seat). Second, I had given up skiing in my teen years, finding it far more enjoyable to join my mother wandering through cozy bookstores than layering up to spend the day going up and down a hill in the frigid snow. Finally, I was scared of heights and falling. In fact, I detested skiing because a vacation that involves that much effort doesn't feel like a vacation to me. I also suck at skiing.[22]

In an effort to hide this (not successfully), I decided to take up snowboarding for the week. Fall after fall, I found myself trying to find balance on this flimsy, very thin board. It took

---

22 As you will discover in this chapter, doing something for a long time doesn't mean you are good at it. I skied for long enough that any reasonable person would be competent at it. I assure you, I am not.

all morning to get down the bunny hill. I would make up an excuse in my lesson every mid-afternoon to go save a table for après ski. What I remember most about the trip is the enthusiasm and love everyone else had for the mountain, the way their stories wove together at that table, and how I felt listening to them. My blah attitude left me on the sidelines of the discussion until I started sharing my missteps and trials of trying to get down the mountain, not by complaining but offering up a play-by-play of my falls.

The approach of shifting the energy and focus to someone else (often the client) is a common misplaced networking technique. The assumption is that your story doesn't matter as much as showing excitement for someone else. This is called a one-way conversation, and after a while it gets boring for everyone. Notice what I did in the conversation by throwing out my not-successful snowboarding attempts? I used humor and my own reality to engage in the conversation. Don't opt yourself out through your own conversation strategy.

Mature networking that attracts stronger colleague relationships and brings you into the mix of conversations and collaborations starts with being solid in who you are and engaging with confidence. Not just listening from the sidelines. By sitting at that table and not talking on our trip to the mountain, I put myself on the sidelines. While these were great friends and there was plenty to talk about besides skiing, whenever the conversation inched toward the slopes, I inched my way out of it. The same thing happens when client conversations inch toward topics you aren't familiar with or aren't in your lane. As you notice yourself inching out of the discussion, ask yourself which part made you want to opt-out and step aside.[23]

---

23 This is making the assumption that the conversations are business-oriented or relatively filled with appropriate small talk. Obviously, if a conversation makes you uncomfortable for inappropriate reasons, don't inch out—get out.

The Fear of Falling (and Being Seen)

Let's face it: it's comfortable to stand a smidge out of the spotlight and let the senior partner take the calls and the responsibility that comes with them. They get the first call about the successes, but also all the fails. They take the wrath of the work not well done and responsibility for answering the complex questions that often come at the most inconvenient times. Yet for many, this spotlight seems to be the epicenter of a well-defined and earned career. To step into this level of responsibility, you have to be ready not just with the expertise and experience, but with a willingness to be seen and understood (even when you don't know the answer or are shockingly wrong).

There is a fear that arises at this point: allowing others to fully see you and your flaws. The nature of a professional services practice, regardless of field (law, accounting, consulting), is that it requires continuous learning and applications which require practice, understanding nuances, possibly getting things wrong or trying something that needs a different solution, and a willingness to collaborate on finding solutions *with* clients rather than *for* them. This level of interaction and engagement in solutions requires your thinking—and the process behind it—to be seen and understood by clients. This level of vulnerability is rarely spoken about. It's also often assumed that the higher you rise in your career, the more confident you are in the work and your position of authority within the field, and so, the more comfortable you are being vulnerable. This assumption, I can assure you, client after client of mine has refuted.

It turns out the higher you rise in your work, the fear of loss or getting it wrong weighs heavier. The focus on covering your bases feels more intense (and is intrinsically part of your job). Yet the advisory role asks that you do the work in a diligent way and provide the accurate and informed advice your clients are looking for.

Consider the toddler learning to ski. I was three years old when my parents strapped skis on my feet. I was five when I was navigating full-day ski school and the lunch line in those mountain restaurants. The falls were often and hard back then, but my little body and immature brain popped right back up and figured out what's next. I figured out what to do to navigate my way down the mountain (even exuding my own version of confidence back in the day). Yet, if you asked me to do the same thing today, I would freeze in fear of getting hurt and the likelihood of impending falls.

Take a new attorney: the falls are often cushioned by the partners and lawyers between them and the client. Step even a bit further into the practice, and the scrutiny of your work and approach becomes that of the client's leaders and the daunting impact of a wrong decision.

In developing a practice, I dare you to find the practitioner who hasn't gotten it wrong a time or two. It's in the recovery from this error that true professionals show up and shine. You need to know how to open a conversation when new knowledge makes your old advice obsolete (or when even more recent advice is simply wrong). You need to know how to make sure your recovery involves ensuring the missteps aren't repeated. And when a client shows up annoyed with something you have done or how you approached a project, understand that their willingness to speak to you about it is a business development opportunity.

Knowing how to prepare the client for the expectations of a strategy and how to communicate expertise without broad-stroke promises of perfection allows the falls to feel a bit more like toddler-Deb falling in the powder of the mountain snow, rather than the harsh falls of adult-Deb trying to snowboard down the mountain.

It's OK to Like What You Do

You know what kept me at that table every afternoon? Watching the pure joy everyone else had for the mountain and their days. They loved it, and it oozed out of them in the banter. Energy and enthusiasm are contagious in conversations, even when someone has no clue what you are talking about. This shows up in small talk and sharing what you love about a hobby, television show, or vacation spot. It also shows up in your work when you can geek out on the nuances in the laws, practice approach, or emerging trends. In other words, remember what you love about what you do; find your joy so you can share it.

Exuding what you love about a practice or the strategies you've been playing around with in your head cannot be replicated. It's uniquely you. It's based on your expertise and experience, as well as your background, values, personality, and approach. You learned it through micro-interactions throughout your life to this point, and it's the value and humanness you bring to the work you do. Nothing can replace this conversation for you.

In our world, a practice can be built on the back of social media, AI, and the strength of an incredible marketing team. But the human component of the business development process asks you to authentically show up. You better understand what your practice looks like when you add up what you're good at and where you find joy and energy in the flow of a practice, project, or case. This equation is a powerful bond in conversations with potential clients, current clients, and colleagues. It is a natural conversation attractor.

Here are a few steps to help you pinpoint what makes you shine:

1. Write a one-sentence description of what you do without fluff.

2. Consider whether this one sentence really spotlights who you are and what you do.

3. Ask yourself: "By reading this one sentence, do I know what I do, and can I tell what I mean by it?" Keep shifting your description of your work until it sounds like you and what you want to be known for right now and going forward.

4. Finally, practice sharing your expertise with someone else. Notice if what you wrote resonates with the other person, or if it still sounds like the one-sentence no-fluff description.

Using this exercise to peel back the layers of you, your expertise, and your personality allows you to find the right words for you and those that resonate with clients. Keep working through this until you can feel the energy align with your professional goals. This is a great starter to remind yourself of what you want to share in meetings with new clients, catching up with old clients, and simply letting colleagues know when to call you.

Choose to Exude Confidence

In studying the professionals who exude confidence, you will start to notice they aren't airbrushed, but unfailingly real and raw in their approach to practice and life. They are willing to share their knowledge with little reservation. They welcome the challenging questions and are steady in their approach to building their network and spotting work (and solutions for clients). They aren't chasing each opportunity at top speed. Instead, they know the appropriate pacing for the moment and the best move (which may be silence and stillness). They also don't lean on generic answers but invest in themselves and clients equally to advise at a level equivalent and worthy of their billable hour. This only comes from confidently knowing and owning who you are and what you do.

Once you build a steady approach, your infectious enthusiasm is the common denominator that can draw clients into your orbit and naturally build your book of business.

The numbers will take care of themselves when you not only recognize what you are known for but believe in it and allow others to see it. While even writing this reeks of vulnerability, allowing clients (and potential clients) to know what you love and care about in your professional life allows them to find that energy as a link to their wants and needs. It's time to remember what's fun about your career and share it unabashedly with others in a way that is seriously infectious.

Case Study: You Really Can Build a Book out of Fun and Games

My client Mike is a great example of building a book out of something you love. While working for a firm that is at the top of the game, he recognized the need for his own business development strategy. Mike laid out a scenario where it felt like his practice was an island in a big firm—with a constant, lonely chase for work, collaborative partners, and clients. He wanted to change that and reinvigorate his career.

Our work together started by shifting the mindset from chasing clients to growing a strong network within the firm. This quickly opened some interesting conversations. One such conversation led to the opportunity to work on cutting-edge technologies—technologies he had worked on when he started his practice more than fifteen years earlier (and which were reminiscent of a childhood passion project). One connection and conversation quickly reminded Mike of what he loves about his practice. Within weeks, he couldn't stop gushing about the work, the strategies involved, and the complexities that make him the one to know within the global firm (as Mike is now introduced by the senior partner when bringing clients to meet him).

Mike is no longer chasing the work but building a steady practice from what he loves. He found his steady pace by stepping back and shifting the view from needing everyone to know and use him to tapping into a network that already existed, expanding it with intention, and being open to the opportunity that was sitting right there. Mike recently shared that he is working longer hours than ever—and has never loved his practice more.

***

When you're in the middle of building your book of business or looking to create a self-sustaining practice, it can be easy to focus on billable hours and marking things off your ever-expanding to-do list. It can be easy to only participate in conversations where you are the expert. But it's important to go back to the basics: remember what you are passionate about, what you love to do. You need to intentionally bring this to the conversation. Yes, the skill set you have built over the years matters, too, but don't underestimate the power of enthusiasm. It's contagious. Without taking this first step, you are simply waiting to be seen.

Your Task List

1. **Remember you are CEO of your practice, and that means being intentional about your Monthly Meetings.** Grab your monthly agenda and add one new entry: "What I loved about this past month." Spend some time filling it in for the first time.

2. **Walk down the halls at work and pause for a conversation or two with colleagues to learn about what they love about what they do.** Swapping stories and hearing different perspectives helps you gather a more robust picture of how various practices complement each other. Ask to be included in others' practice group meetings, not just to share your work, but to focus on where your work overlaps.

3. **Take five minutes and make a list of all the work you love to do.** See how specific and nuanced you can get within this timeframe. If this is challenging, go back and think about what you loved in high school or college. Tap into this energy like a power source for the business you are cultivating for yourself.

Allow Your Practice to Be Seen

*Getting picked for the work requires others
to know about you and what you do.*

I can still remember the first marked copy of an executive summary I received back as an intern and the horror of realizing this was part of a job. Fifteen years of training built a resilience to feedback on drafts or my work ideas. In fact, part of my business development approach entails leaning into the feedback and ideas of others to build something stronger. I thought I was good with letting others analyze me and the work I do, until the launch date of my first book. Holding my finger above the keyboard, I sat on the phone not quite ready to release the book into the world. A member of my book team noticed my hesitation and proclaimed, "Oh, you are human."

Until that point, I had turned redlines and drafts like I was closing the next big deal. I read feedback and focused on making the manuscript the best it could be. Yet publishing a book meant people were going to read my work without me being able to gauge (or adjust my work) based on their feedback. My work was going to be seen, and I could no longer control by whom. I wish I could tell you that I worry less at this point in my career, but I would be lying. I learned that taking that leap to let your work be seen and known by others is the step not just into exponential growth, but into allowing others to know what you do—which provides the groundwork for exponential growth, and the self-sustaining practice we've been talking about.

What You Love About What You Do

Sure, it may seem easy to focus on what's not working or what needs to change before you make yourself known. In reality, the easiest way to get comfortable with allowing others to see you and your work is to focus on what you love about it and the immense value you bring. Said another way, lean into your strengths and let them shine.

To put this into practice, let's geek out on what you love. Answer the following questions as fast as possible. If it helps, grab a colleague or two and make it a speed round with everyone answering these two questions over and over again, until you are simply exhausted by the exercise and possibly enlightened by what you learn about yourself (and your colleagues).

1. The most fun I have in my practice is: _____

2. I love it when clients ask me: _____

Now that you have these answered, let's use them. Match what you love with the skills you bring to the professional world. Based on your answers, consider what skills you have built that support the fun projects and questions you love. Which of these are necessary for lots of the work you do? These are skills that are continually needed by your clients today and those you might be working with tomorrow. Most likely, it won't be specific knowledge of a law or business model (they change) or a particular company (they change, too). Look deeper. Consider the skills and expectations clients have for the highest level of strategy and support from you. This will allow you to find your new base, which can help you regroup and reimagine your career, as necessary.

The Power in Knowing What You're Known For

When it comes to getting out there and being known, you may think of chasing the latest trends, of being the loudest in the room, or otherwise creating a whole lot of hoopla for you and your practice. But that's not what it's about (at least at first). Knowing what you are known for—that's your secret sauce. What is the foundation of your practice? It starts with your unique expertise that allows you to build, tweak, and navigate in a continuous loop, creating endless variations for clients.

And it's something you've been building and fine-tuning over the years, whether you realize it or not.

If you've been on this journey for a while, you may recall the timeline exercise from *After Hello*. The exercise walks you through identifying the people you've met and the lessons learned from your first job until today. It's the foundation of your work and what gives your expertise a unique approach that simply cannot be copied by others.[24]

In other words, what you're known for is more than a resume. The power of a sophisticated practice is the blend of knowledge, expertise, and style. And it takes a keen eye to spot it. To get started, consider:

---

24 The timeline exercise can be found in the book resources: https://debfeder.com/clients.

1. What are three specific examples of substantive work that clients come to you with over and over again?

2. How would you describe how you do this work? How is it unique to you and your practice?

3. How would your best clients describe the value of your work to others?

4. What do your clients appreciate about you and your work style?[25]

The substantive core of your work isn't always obvious. That's why the first question gets you thinking of the work everyone will always need (not just what they come to you for right now). Again, this won't always be aspects of the work itself, which can change on a whim. It might be how you work through changes, your background in understanding the industry's evolution, or your ability to communicate the minutiae to a client. Notice the blend of what you love to do and the steady work and approach clients can count on.

Using these questions as a guide, you can train yourself to focus on what works and what is appreciated, in addition to highlighting the full package that clients get by selecting you as the trusted advisor. The answers to these questions will also help as you practice entering new conversations—reconnecting with colleagues, for example. Take a confident deep breath and talk about a project you are working on in a way that is interesting to others, looking for intersection points where your passion aligns with their interest or needs.

---

25 From time to time, I am involved in these discussions with clients. Hearing what they love about their advisors is kind of like listening to a work hug. It is awesome and almost always valuable information because they see you differently than you see yourself (said another way, you are your own worst critic. How do those who choose to work with you value your work?)

And remember, it's also the approach and humanness you bring to work. Quality clients are not simply looking for your ability to read and interpret the laws. They're also looking for critical thinking skills and a strategic mindset that can apply to a variety of circumstances to help them pick the best next step. They also want, and desperately need, someone by their side as the calm in the storm and a steady hand to dig in and find creative solutions to their biggest problems.

Empty Expertise Shows Up Sooner or Later

We live in a world where everyone can proclaim themselves an expert. All you've got to do is post confident-sounding videos, provide an inspiring story, amass a following, and you have the authority to tell others what to do. Right? Wrong. This is simply noise. It lacks the depth clients are looking for when it comes to advisors. That's why you've got to differentiate yourself; to know how to navigate and be at the forefront of what's next; to know not only how to work through a challenge but find the opportunity hiding inside of it.

Social media somehow makes everyone feel like they can be an expert, even though they don't know enough to contribute to higher-level conversations. You can't fake expertise with a high-gloss, low-content approach. In other words, it's not the overly processed pitch or the glossy yet generic materials that signal expertise to high-quality clients; rather, it's the interesting discussions and smaller conversational moments that allow a client to connect with you. It's the nuances of your expertise that address their specific questions.

Another obstacle social media has created is the feeling that expertise has a certain look—that you've got to have the sunny interview in a high-back chair, a podcast, or a perfectly cultivated content plan before you can speak to clients and colleagues about your work. Don't fall into the trap of trying to look like another influencer. Often the least gloss is the most attractive to the best clients.

Recently, at a firm workshop, a newer attorney suggested that her LinkedIn profile was in the early stages, that the content had not caught up to her expertise, so it was not yet ready for a soft launch with clients. With a smidge of a smile, I assured her that a professional expertise plan doesn't need the base of an Instagram profile with its perfectly cultivated content board. The goal is not a beautiful checkerboard of posts that are all "on brand." Rather, you want a place for clients and colleagues to confirm the depth of your expertise and to see that it matches what you are proclaiming, as you gather up new business and offer your services to clients.

Focus on you, your clients, and the true base of your expertise—the way you jump into projects, commit to the end of the work, know the industry, or know stuff because you've done it. It may not be as flashy, but it works. Why? Because fake expertise shines as a dim light flashing on and off in the dark, like a flashlight gone bad.

My in-house connections and clients often reflect on the rampant amount of empty expertise pitching them every day. Mark, an in-house attorney, lamented about the number of contacts from attorneys or legal technologist "experts" who assured him they were the solution he was looking for to transform not only his department, but the way they served the company. Yet it only took one or two simple questions to prove how little expertise they really had.

They assumed that the speed and wits of a "solution" would be bright enough to get them in the door. Yet, the corporate needs required a depth of knowledge that couldn't come from an app. It required a nuanced understanding of the subject matter and business acumen to guide the appropriate technology solutions. Mark wasn't willing to settle for anything less than what he had always expected from the legal teams he managed and hired: subject matter experts, with emotional intelligence to navigate senior meetings and relationships, and a willingness to be continuous learners. Technology couldn't replace any of this.

Case Study: Audrey and The Quest for a Bigger Practice

Let's take the story of Audrey. Audrey had worked for years in a big, reputable law firm, building her practice by showing up and doing the work that her litigation department was known for. A high-profile case seemed like an incredible opportunity, and she jumped in. However, the case went on for years, making Audrey feel pigeonholed in her expertise, only getting to do the work of this one case, in this one way, for this one client.

Audrey reached out to me wanting to give her practice some legs. She wanted to figure out a way to navigate into other work that could allow her to use her expertise and expand what she's known for, recognizing that her practice and its future depended on more than this one project. Audrey felt like she was sitting at that table watching everyone else develop practices. She wanted to be in the mix.

While Audrey viewed this situation as an insurmountable calamity, I offered a different view.

First, the feeling of being stuck and underappreciated is valid and understandable in the middle of a long-term commitment that seems to be simmering for an unhealthy period of time. Second, it was time to start recognizing the gifts and options the opportunity had provided (otherwise they would get lost in the intense desire to expand the practice immediately). Getting the chance to work at a deeper level offered its own gifts. It allowed Audrey to know the client team and understand how to build a bigger relationship with a client. Doing the project many times allowed her to build efficiencies in the process, understand the nuances between each variation, and cultivate an expertise that wouldn't have been possible if she had only done the task once.

Now, this doesn't mean I didn't understand or appreciate Audrey's concerns about what's next for her practice and wanting to expand her options. But it was important to point out the alternatives and gifts it provided before moving forward. Appreciating what's been done up to this point makes it easier to know how to navigate the next steps (and see the holes in your strategy). Audrey is doing this work, and so can you.

Show What You Know

What you've learned through experience—what you now know—impacts the work you bring in and the wisdom you contribute to client questions.

So, what is it you know?

To get you started, pick a significant project from your years of practice, and consider these prompts:

1. What substantive experience did it provide you?

2. Next, make a new list of all that it allowed you to experience in building, growing, and nurturing relationships (both internal and external).

3. Finally, make a list of the skills and strategies you picked up along the way. These are more procedural. They might be how you managed a project, work opportunities you spotted off the main project, or what it evolved into.

4. Consider all the ways you might showcase what you've learned through this exercise: weave it into an introduction, craft a LinkedIn post, share it in a keynote or panel conversation, or simply share it as part of the banter before a client picks you for the next project.

Understanding the nuances in what you know allows you to pull out the portions that continue to excite you, versus those you'd rather leave behind. Leaning into it, one piece at a time, allows you to build something beyond the billable hour, a practice that is sustainable over the course of a career. Because it's more than a one-line resume description. This focus allows you to shape the narrative around your practice and what you offer to clients as the advisor they want to know (and use).

The goal isn't to start jumping through hoops for each and every new, shiny project or try to wrap your expertise into the package a client wants in a way that doesn't really sound like you. Instead, you want to find the nuggets that are transformational for you and your career and learn how to translate that to clients.

Spot Misaligned Work

Want to know what the awkward twist looks like when you try to change your work to match what others are looking to hire in a way that doesn't really align with you and your work?

Do a quick scroll through LinkedIn and you'll see many a professional jumping too fast too soon, looking for the next best thing at every turn. These include announce-ments such as, "Now I am working on…" or updates that happen way too frequently or feel like they came out of left field and have no alignment with the work you thought they were known for. Sometimes this is intentional and often it is grasping to look like they're on top of a hot new trend. Now, look at your own LinkedIn profile and ask whether it reflects your practice today and how you want others to know about your work when making that first call. Does your practice, and the story around it, feel consistent and steady, with good growth—or more like it's jumping around with a whole lot of empty information?

***

It's often a welcome distraction to hop from place to place, group to group, or to continuously tweak the ideal client profile. Yet the challenge evolves into a deeper, better space when you can stick with the boring parts and drudge through the obstacles. While not the most exciting, it ultimately allows you to have a depth of expertise reserved for those who went the extra mile. It's easy to chase the shiny new thing, especially when you arrive at this pivot point with an uncomfortable feeling that maybe you waited a bit too long to start navigating the next portion of your professional journey. The need to catch up is a pretty awful feeling that can drive you to chase something shiny rather than stay focused on a longer-term result.

One of the biggest challenges when navigating this stage of your career is to hold still and be seen. Discomfort with being known and allowing others to see not just your expertise but your enthusiasm, often gets in the way of allowing the client connections to evolve. Trust me when I tell you that there's less nail biting as each draft and project comes along. Doing the projects and deepening your expertise helps. Using that as the base is an awesome launching point to build your practice and attract the right fit clients that energize and excite you.

This unique combination that you've put together to this point, combined with your steady approach to what clients want and need, is the secret sauce that only you can offer. The magic is allowing it to help you connect with your clients, colleagues, and community to create exponential results. This connection happens when you not only show up and answer the call but step up and offer advice that clients are looking for and help them move closer to their goals because of your involvement.

Your Task List

1. **Pretend you are a reporter writing a story about you and your practice.** What would your introduction paragraph be that allows others to know your own unique qualities, expertise, and approach? Notice how much you write about the parts of work you love and love being known for.

2. **It's time for your Monthly Meeting.** Grab your calendar and map out four times over the next year where you are going to intentionally share your practice and expertise with others. These might be speaking engagements, contributing to an article, or planned LinkedIn content. Getting strategic about the pacing of your content plan allows it to be impactful.

3. **Pick someone you respect in another field (or even an influencer on social media).** When you strip away the gloss, what makes their work respectable? Make a list of all that stands out to you and consider one way you can translate this into your practice.

Employ the Polite Permission Slip

You need to find out how ready your clients are for new ideas before you start tossing them their way.

When I was little, rarely a month went by that you didn't hear a tapping on the wall or something being dragged across the floor in the middle of the night. Our family room was my mother's canvas for constantly moving furniture, rearranging family photos on the great big wall, or rethinking the flow of traffic from the front door to the kitchen. This was my mother's secret gift, and something she taught me about creating a welcoming space. As we grew into adulthood, she would come into our homes and move stuff around, which was a jarring experience for her two sons-in-law. Recognizing that it wasn't going over all that well, my mother started pausing to suggest the change before shoving the chair (or table) into its new spot. This simple pause gave them the opportunity to opt-in to the change. Rarely did they stop her from executing her great idea that helped make their space a more comfortable and approachable home.

Now, I must admit that I have taken this lesson and like to move furniture and shift things around for the flow of company and conversation. I am less likely to do this in my home (although it happens) but am often found moving a table, podium, or projector when setting up at an event venue before a speaking engagement, workshop, or retreat. How do I do this without throwing off an entire events team? I don't avoid it. But I make it predictable by casually mentioning it as part of our event planning to ensure it is an anticipated part of my workshop secret sauce. Part of the success of my programs is the ability for participants to feel welcome and engage with each other. Room design plays a big part in making this happen. I might be known to turn on music and make everyone have a bit of a dance party as we optimize the room flow. Yet before I engage in this room design, I cannot change one thing in that room that others have carefully put together without a positive nod from them in advance. The civil nature of this approach softens the changes that are about to be offered up and indicates how wide the door is open to ideas.

The same approach also works wonders in shifting client conversations (either current or prospective) from one-sided monologues that are seeking alignment to mutually participatory discussions that ask for permission upfront to offer advice and ideas. It starts by asking: *How open is that person to hearing a different perspective or a solution they simply haven't thought of yet?* When you can figure that out, new ideas emerge. Problem-solving then takes on a much deeper dimension, often with far better results.

Start With Their Viewpoint

When it comes to bringing your expertise to the table, clients want specific advice. But nobody likes a know-it-all. Instead, you need to understand exactly what they want and then make sure you are moving your advice from all possible and permissible options to realistic choices (maybe just one or two) that you think are best and an explanation of why you think this is the best start in making a good decision.

The first step: understanding your client's viewpoint. I break this down (literally asking them to tell you more about their expertise, experience, ideas, and challenges) in *Tell Me More*. Within that stage of the conversation, you are learning and building trust with the client. Respecting their perspective, you can make sure your response has maturity and careful thought, which turns generic advice into something that considers the full picture.

Before you can give the full extent of your advice as a trusted thinking partner, another shift must happen. You need to get the initial permission to not just tell them what is possible (all the options) but what you recommend.

First, you need to gain clarity and permission upfront for the scope of advice the client is looking for. There is nothing more annoying than getting a fifty-state survey in a big chart when you asked whether Iowa allows you to pay parking tickets by credit card. (OK, this example is far too simplistic for everything you do, but you get the point.) If the initial goal does not involve annoying the client, then understanding the exact question and how they want the answer is a necessity.

Take a step back and consider if the strategy they want to build is looking at the question or project from the right view. Pause to make sure you and the client are on the same page. If you get this wrong, you risk not only annoyance but giving bad advice.

This plays out every day:

- **An Everyday Example:** You're shopping for a car, and a salesperson overshares details on a car and its five hundred benefits that you couldn't care less about. They didn't gauge what you were interested in upfront and didn't align their suggestions to your particular concerns.

- **My Personal Example:** I recently needed to hire an outside resource to provide a few simple tools for my business. I had a clear list of what I was looking for. I knew the budget for these items, and it should have been a few thousand dollars and about three weeks of work. The proposal I received? A one-year contract for over six figures that didn't include my punch list but was instead what the company representative assured me was really the necessary step. Not only was it a misalignment, but the disregard for the permission granted spoke volumes about what the possible working relationship would look like. (Yeah, it didn't happen.)

- **A Professional Service Example:** A company reaches out for advice on a niche situation that impacts one of their business lines. They need an answer this week on the best course of action. What do they get? A memo outlining all of the options, in all of the states, for all of the businesses, with not one piece of advice given. This results in the real work landing back on the desk of the in-house attorney. Yeah, that situation didn't work out all that well either.

Before you jump into action (which is what most people do), know what questions need to be asked upfront and the best approach to get this information to the clients. This permission slip is the first of many if you want to build a quality client relationship that demonstrates not just your immense expertise, but your investment in building a thriving client relationship.

If you've read any of my prior books, you might recall Matilda. Matilda is a litigator, which means she is rarely involved in establishing a client's corporate strategy. Yet, she will tell you that understanding how a company is structured and how the company's broader goals impact not just the litigation strategy, but her approach to advising clients on the smallest questions they bring to her each day. If she shut herself off to these questions or conversations by simply referring them to someone in her corporate department, for example, then her advice wouldn't be half as good as it is. Nor would she be seen as the partner clients view her to be. This is the reputation Matilda carries with her. It starts with caring deeply, then taking that care and translating it into learning all she can, to enrich her advice and strategy. Matilda gets the permission slip by investing in knowing more. So, when she offers advice, the clients know she was paying attention and it's worth listening to. Those clients also understand that Matilda will carry this care and expectation to every other advisor she brings into the project with her.

Don't Just Shout Out Your Ideas

In the hustle of getting that task marked off your long list of to-dos, it's tempting to just throw advice or answers at clients, hoping it will expedite the next step. Instead, you need to slow down and make sure your client is paying attention to your wisdom, and that you have permission to narrow down the answer from what's possible to what's suggested. And that requires a pause in the conversation.

This is where the next permission slip comes into play (and takes your advisory role up a notch). To get your advice heard, the client needs it to be told to them differently. Enter: *Might I Suggest*.

Now, if *Might I Suggest* isn't your tone (or approach), here are a few other ways to say the same thing:

- Something you might consider...
- Just throwing it out there...
- Can we brainstorm this?
- I don't know if you've thought of...
- Another thing I was thinking...
- There is another option to consider...

(What else would you add to this list?)

You might try a few out until you figure out which one works best for (and sounds like) you and connects with your clients. Texting a formal general counsel a note that says, "Just bouncing ideas around in my head," might not land the way you are hoping it will. But picking up the phone and offering, "I have been considering the conversation from earlier and I see two viable paths that get you to where you need to be within the next month," might open a much better conversation.

Might I Suggest often feels a bit risky, because it is. Putting yourself and your expertise out there means you are standing behind the plan. This is why we talked about owning your ideas and expertise first. But remember, clients are hiring you to eventually provide the strategy they should follow, not just provide a map filled with every possible avenue they could consider (throwing the work right back on their plate).

This level of advice doesn't happen on the first day of practice but builds through experience, project by project, throughout your career. It also requires you to know the client just as well as you know your expertise (like Matilda does) and to understand them.[26] Sure, you can hand your research department the notes and ask them to send you a summary. That's part of it. But understanding the nuances and perspective of your particular client (talking about the human that hired you at the company) requires you to get into those conversations and pay attention to what they are saying and the reasoning behind the project at hand.

Here's what we have done so far:

1. A client comes to you with a question or conversation.

2. You develop and grasp the background enough so that you both understand the scope of the question.

3. The client grants permission for the scope.

4. You do the work (well).

5. You bring your advice and the bigger answer to the client.

6. You shift from all the possibilities to your informed advice.

This is where *Might I Suggest* becomes extremely useful. This one phrase puts a pause in the conversation and gets the client's attention. Using this moment, you can set the stage for why you are making a recommendation. Your advice at this point is best informed by your understanding of them,

---

26 Yup, you need to download *Know Your Client* and start working through the guide.

the company, and all the priorities and considerations that need to be wrapped into this one piece of strategic direction. It may seem like a lot, but let me tell you, it's worth it.

In the middle of the conversation, all these pieces flow rather quickly. Breaking it down helps you pause and practice, so you don't miss a step. Speaking of which, the best way to practice this strategy is with your colleagues. As you talk through a project or case, pause, offer that you have an idea, and insert your suggestion. It could be an approach to a project, or simply an idea for lunch. Either option works when you start making this intentional pause a part of your conversation and relationship strategy.

There are endless scenarios in which *Might I Suggest* helps move the conversation forward through a willingness to offer concrete ideas. Let's focus on a few specific, yet common examples:

Scenario: Internal Permission to Be Involved in the Transition

One particularly sensitive space to employ this strategy is when you are involved in a client relationship transition. When a partner starts to see retirement on the horizon, it's not uncommon to start talking to another partner or two (or three) about taking over the client relationships that have been built up over the years. This initial conversation often starts to generate excitement for the new partner. Once you start to calculate the numbers, business generation goals suddenly aren't completely out of reach. But there is one common story right after this first conversation: nothing. It isn't discussed, the client relationship remains the same, the senior partner is still working as much as before, and there is zero mention of a timeline to make this happen. All of this leaves the heir apparent watching, wondering, and worrying about what to do next.

The way forward is to start engaging in conversations and strategies with the senior partner. Not in some sort of weird nagging way, but from time to time, check in and make suggestions on the mutual nurturing of the client. Do it in such a way that keeps you involved in a manner the senior partner is comfortable with and considers the broader client relationship.[27]

Scenario: Breaking the Friend Barrier

Part of the complication of building a professional practice is that all those years in school and the initial years of practice provided the ripe opportunity to make friends through the common misery of figuring everything out. Late-night study groups and due diligence sessions lead to knowing more about your colleagues than can ever be found out at a networking event. But careers and lives change, and people head their separate ways. This leaves you with friends all over the place, doing interesting things, often related or connected to your work, but in different venues. What's left: lots of friends you love and appreciate. While you don't want to do anything to ruin that friendship, it would be awesome to be doing business with them. When it comes to priorities, friendship wins. However, it feels like walking away from a missed opportunity to not at least offer up the idea of joining forces and forging a new work relationship, as a client-advisor. Now, the big question: how to make this happen in a way that isn't weird?

---

27 While I could talk about client transitions and the evolution of a practice being handed down within a firm, the key here is communication (early and often).

This business development conversation seems fraught with complications. *Might I Suggest* allows you to carefully offer up your expertise without overstepping and possibly damaging a friendship. There are two steps to this strategy:

- First, allow a business conversation to take place. Simply letting a friend or colleague know that you want to ask them a business question puts a pin in your conversation (or lunch) that you don't just want to catch up on the gossip and family news but want to pivot into work. This is often just enough of a mention to allow everyone to eagerly shift the topics covered.

- Second, you need to listen and learn (by staying curious).[28] Focus on all they are doing while being actively interested. Jumping right into "*Might I Suggest* we work together," is not a great approach. *Might I Suggest* (probably a less formal version would be better with a friend), and brainstorming ideas based on what you know of your friend and what they're focused on right now, allows you to take your friendship and move it (not leave it behind) to the worktable. The very best advisory relationships share friendship or camaraderie as their foundation. Don't be afraid of it but gently look for the openings (like when they complain about a work problem). And if the opening is not enthusiastically responded to, don't push it.

Scenario: Open an Opportunity Through Gratitude

Have you noticed where an athlete heads right after the victory? To pause and share a moment with the team that made it happen. This is often coaches, loved ones, and teammates.

---

28 Yup. This is the cornerstone of my curious conversation strategy.

They aren't standing around ignoring everyone, pretending like the victory was a solo mission. Use this lesson and bond with clients over the work you just accomplished together and share your gratitude for the opportunity to be included.

If you ask me, the one business development and client nurturing strategy to lean on when you have limited time and can do nothing else is to say thank you to someone each day. One, it's good practice. There is abundant evidence of the positive results from a practice of gratitude; it's kindness in action, and a great door opener for what's next.

In that quick conversation expressing appreciation for being involved in a case, project, or deal, pause and ask the client to share what's next for the implementation of their priorities. Lean back on *Tell Me More* and then use a well-placed pause and a *Might I Suggest* as a place to offer up your perspective based on everything you've learned in the work you just finished. This is an opening to exchange ideas. Rather than pitch or start work, it's a time to be insightful. Again, this isn't about the billable hour. It's about true engagement with the client that allows you to be involved in more than the "transactional work" for the client.

This also works in the smallest of conversations. If a client calls with a quick question, get curious about what's behind the question. If you are finishing a team meeting, pause and ask what else everyone is working on. If the client call ends a few minutes early (yes, it happens from time to time), ask them to stick around for you to say thanks for including you and ask a good question that allows your advice to show up and shine through without needing a formal invitation or meeting set up. Use your small moments to show up and, in a conversational tone that matches the flow of a client conversation, be willing to share your ideas that are within the scope of what the client is looking for. Be the advisor that simply bounces ideas, joins the conversation, and allows it to be enough because the big work follows.

Case Study: Get Everyone on Board for Lunch

Do you remember my client Jack from *Tell Me More*? Jack is diligent in building relationships within the firm and with clients. He came to me to discuss how to balance not overstepping in a client relationship while carefully ensuring he didn't miss any client development opportunities. You see, most of his work was with clients dispersed throughout the country, yet he wanted to focus on cultivating local client relationships. He recognized that the shift from keeping in touch with clients by phone and email to planning something in-person requires a smidge of intentional planning (and team coordination). In addition, as part of a larger client team, Jack was cognizant of not wanting to overstep his role with the internal team.

We discussed the nurturing phase of the relationships and the careful dance of not wanting to leapfrog over any part-ners while demonstrating care and investment in the client relationship. The decision: get permission for a client meal with everyone. A quick email with the suggestion instantly moved the partners into action.

Now, you might think it stinks to come up with the idea, offer it up, and have others take over the invitations and plans, but that is simply short-sighted. Jack wasn't worried about who put the idea out there; he just wanted to make it happen. He wanted to continue building the client relation-ships with the other partners without worrying that he had left an opportunity on the table. The collaborative approach requires trust and not chasing credit (either for the idea or in origination numbers). It's simply caring about good client relationships.

Jack continues to keep his eye on what matters. He's built a book filled with clients who align with his practice, created strong internal relationships, and stays top of mind as the trusted advisor because he not only picks up the phone but will linger a couple of times a year when everyone intentionally pauses to get together and sit down for lunch.

Show Your Team How It's Done

As your practice matures, making sure your team not only understands the value of *Might I Suggest* but puts it into practice allows you to confidently bring in more business, knowing clients will be cared for and respected in the same way you practice each and every day. The best way is not to sit in a room and tell everyone to be responsive and respectful; it is to model it. By allowing teams to practice it and by continuously looping back to discuss how to enrich the total client relationship with your whole team, you create a culture of investment in the client relationship and in being the advisors they want and need.

As a member of a client team, consider all the ways *Might I Suggest* allows you to learn more and deepen the client work:

- **Create shadow opportunities.** We learn by watching not just the work getting done, but the client relationship being built. Show new team members not only how you show interest in client projects but how you offer up ideas and suggestions on issues.

- **See the next project.** When team members are working with the clients on particular aspects of a project, make sure there is a "what's next" touch base. *Might I Suggest* comes from knowing about upcoming projects and handling the lingering questions.

- **Ask for ideas.** Pause before ending team meetings and ask what everyone sees in upcoming client engagements and what advice needs to be shared. Generating a culture of brainstorming and collaborative client support gives oxygen and energy to your suggested advice and ideas. The next step is to make a plan for the client to talk through the advice and make sure they know the whole team is invested in the advisory role.

The most frequent situation where ideas and client relationships get stuck is when team members are uncertain of their roles or worried about overstepping. This is a frequent question about getting permission to nurture a relationship on a client team when you are not the client relationship manager. The answer to this is easy: as the CEO of your practice, if you don't have permission, seek out a conversation to explain the relationship and your goal to strengthen it for the whole team. If you are the relationship manager, set up a plan to coordinate client nurturing efforts so that the client has a feel-good relationship with everyone on your team. If you cling to the relationship and don't let anyone in, you are going to have to do all the nurturing or risk the client finding others who outwardly care more. In addition, allowing new relationships to form throughout the client team is just another case where the glue is getting stickier between you, your team, and the client relationships you want to blossom.

A Note on Team Alignment

When breaking down where something went wrong on a team or with a client communication, it's because the way you talk about the approach is vague at best, with everyone in the room nodding in agreement, without actually coming to an understanding of what this looks like in practice. Want an example? Ask everyone on your team what it looks like for them to get something to the client by the end of the week. Or what "client-ready" looks like. The goal is not to be exasperated when others don't share your vision, but to work together toward a clear, shared understanding that is simple to execute.

Thinking you can manage everything for everyone for all scenarios is not only exhausting but also limits your practice and its ability to grow. Rethinking how you use your team, build trust in client communications, and allow for a collaborative advisory relationship is where you not only build what's next but also allow the exponential results to happen when everyone wins together (most especially the client from the benefit of a whole team of invested advisors).

***

Advising a client often feels like walking a tightrope of not wanting to step outside the safe space for fear of falling (or worse, getting replaced). Slow down and allow yourself to find a wider space in which to operate by opening the conversation with *Hello*. Learn more about the client and their expectations and goals. From there you can start offering better suggestions. *Might I Suggest* is your door opener (for current clients needing advice and potential clients looking to pick the right advisor who is already scheming with ideas to solve their problems). When you and your team are dedicated to using this "polite permission slip" before offering advice, great things can happen. Especially when it is followed by some really strong ideas.

Your Task List

1. **If you could give clients one piece of advice, what would it be?** Take some time to brainstorm this question and consider how it shows up in your work. Is it positively impacting a client's experience working with you and does your advice add value?

2. **As CEO, it is important that you are empowering your team to support a common goal.** Pick one member of your team and loop them into a client relationship you're focused on right now. Brainstorm how the two of you can work on this together.

3. **Who else on your team needs to understand your clients as well as you do?** What conversations have you had with them to learn what they know? What conversations can you help get them experience with in the coming months?

Practice Giving Good Options

Once you have the opening to help a client make a decision, you need to be ready to offer up your advice.

Let me tell you about ordering dinner around my house. Negotiations between family members around what sounds good often leave me more exhausted than studying for a con law exam. When I finally arrive at tacos, it feels as though someone should make a public declaration of my expedient and successful negotiation strategy, until my husband jumps in, hears the plan, and asks, "Did no one want sushi tonight?" Reopening the discussion causes confusion and, in truth, hostility, as I feel my triumph being stripped away.

I used to think it was just me. Yet after many client conversations, I find that's not the case. The begrudgery over the number of decisions asked of you influences how you feel about making decisions that seem extraneous. To build the book of business you want, you must be willing to show up and offer your opinion so clients can make choices armed with your expertise, experience, and an understanding of where they are headed. Clients want you to speak up at the table and offer not just all the ideas but also be able to explain what you believe to be the best options, and why. They want to have a strategy discussion with you. They want their questions answered with the depth of someone who doesn't just know the work but can explain it and hash out the ideas in real-time. The key? Make sure your advice isn't in a professional vacuum. It needs to feel insightful and informed based on the client's industry, business model, and bigger institutional goals.[29]

Similar to dinner, some of the decisions clients face aren't that complex, but the sheer volume of information gets in the way of knowing what option is best. Other decisions have nuances layered on top of each other that make strategic advisors helpful in looking at the layers and brainstorming the very best approach. And when it comes to a trial or complex negotiations, the advisor needs to be the one putting together the plan to put it into action. With each of these scenarios, the best advisors stay in the room and don't just dump all the information and the decisions on the client and then run away. They stay a part of the process and give their best advice with confidence.

I often hear grumblings on both sides: from advisors—how much advice to give, wanting to weigh in with help on decisions, but not sure how to give it; and from clients—there's a dire need to change how advice is given ("if you aren't giving me real options and advice, you're just adding more work to my plate"). To make the value proposition of outside professional advisors work, the advice needs to be specific,

---

29 This is how you show your expertise and how well you pay attention. If you fail to do so, your advice will likely be met with total disregard for all the prep, planning, and state of the business as the client rolls their eyes and reaches for their Rolodex to start finding a new team. Trust me.

actionable, feasible, and aligned.[30] As one of my clients put it, "If I don't give my clients the strategy I think is best, they will fire me and go find someone who will."

What Elevated Advice Looks Like

When you're working to be a trusted advisor, you can't just call people up and announce, "I'm ready to be trusted by you. Bring me all the things and I will take care of you!" That's not only wildly weird, it's also an immature assumption that clients want a proclamation, rather than proof of your ability to be in that advisory role. Just like most great mentorships are never "announced" but evolve between professionals, the same holds true for trusted advisory relationships. It's rare for there to be a formal proclamation; instead, it's seen in the work that comes your way. Since your business model relies on these types of relationships, you must be ready to expand your role when you recognize the door is open after asking, *Might I Suggest*. It's important to consider what elevated advice looks like for these big relationships:

1. **It's specific.** Clients are begging for good advice that doesn't have a generic look and feel. They want to make sure their unique business model, priorities, industry trends, and approach are accounted for. That means the more specific the ideas and options you throw out, the more likely they will be well-received (or at least considered).

---

30 This is important for partners to train associates in and model—not just the advice being given, but how you narrow it down and present it. Being able to practice this along the way is way better than being thrown into the fire. And if you are the associate, ask to learn more about this (a little reverse of *Tell Me More*).

2. **It's actionable.** Make sure your options and advice can be acted on by the client with relative ease. Ask yourself what it would take to move forward with Option A or Option B. If you can't figure it out, they probably can't either. When offering options, think through the next steps that the client needs to consider and contemplate the impact of what happens next.

3. **It's feasible.** Since you have been getting to know the client and how it aligns with your practice and expertise, narrowing down the ideas and strategies to those that can actually be implemented is an excellent start. Something that is far-fetched, unreasonable, or doesn't take into account resource allocations will lose its luster (and your trust) quickly.

4. **It's aligned.** After being specific, this might feel repetitive, but it takes what you know about the client into account and makes sure your advice is consistent with the goals, priorities, and approach they need. If it's a risk-averse company (or in an industry requiring a heightened sensitivity to risk right now), then offering the bold, hyper-risky ideas without addressing the reason you think it will work will come off as ill-informed and misguided. If the client is in a hurry and your advice is that you will come back to them in the next few weeks with ideas, you are probably not going to last long on that client team. The best way to confirm alignment is a conversation.

Making Decisions Takes Practice

Since decisions seem to be things that are avoided, my suggestion is to practice them on something much lower stakes than client conversations. Let's go back to talking about dinner.

Practice knowing your options: what food do you have available? How much time do you have?

Practice narrowing your choices: if you can only pick two things, what are they?

Practice being specific: don't just speak in categories; what do you actually want?

Practice advocating for the right choice: make a speech like you are running for student council advocating for the dinner option (or two to choose from).

Finally, enjoy the satisfaction of a meal that was based on logic, solid analysis, good choices, and a final decision.

Clients Crave Help in Making Complex Decisions

Most of the work that lands on the decision maker's desk that needs outside support is far more complex than "Yes" or "No." It has nuances and needs that need to be analyzed from various perspectives. While the legal framework is one lens, it also needs to consider the business priorities and goals. Helping people get to "Yes" is often much more appreciated than you know. This doesn't mean saying, "Yes," when the answer is, "No." But if your automatic response is, "No," you'll sound like a bossy parent who's shutting off communication with their kids, even though you're doing it to stay safe.

It's also a faulty assumption to think that your piece of advice is of no consequence. Assume that if they are paying you to weigh in, it matters.

On top of wanting help in making decisions, clients want your confident contributions. Merely shelling out advice of all the possibilities does little to help them get the work moving forward, one way or another. It's kind of like listing off all the aisles in the grocery store when trying to figure out that dinner plan.

A practical exercise in testing this out is to pick a project on your desk and ask yourself if you know exactly what is being asked of you. Ways to test this are to consider whether you are giving all the options in the universe, or the strategic advice clients are looking for. Do you have a clear directive from the client or colleague team on what they want? Consider asking for clarification right here as a good first step in making decisions and contributing something more concrete to the work requested.

What's Holding You Back?

Before insisting that you start offering big, bold options to clients, it's critical to acknowledge what's keeping you from this in the first place.

First, as an outside advisor there is a sense of duty and responsibility to get something "right." This quest leaves you trying to uncover all options and scenarios before moving forward and sharing the work product. Here's the key: it isn't necessarily about being "right," but understanding "ready," the point where you've done the work to make sure you are giving sound advice that is aligned with the client's expectations. Thankfully, as your practice matures, that point when the work is "ready" becomes clearer.

Second, making a decision that doesn't feel like yours to make feels risky. Just like you are asking clients for permission to show up and give the advice, you are waiting for clients to invite you to the conversation and open the door for you to help make a decision. With both parties waiting for the proper invitation, it seems like a complicated game of professional "chicken." Rather than be the one who is always waiting, gain clarity upfront. This will give you the permission and scope of representation and expectation for decisions going forward. Oftentimes, this is done best project by project. As you grow in your position, the likelihood that clients want real advice from you is pretty strong. The longer you work with clients, the easier it is to find this line faster.

Case Study: Being Decisive Can Give You Back Your Time and Energy

Meet my client, Heather. Heather has a C-suite position in a growing company and has worked with me on setting priorities and managing the growth for a few years. One of her biggest challenges is getting others on board with an idea or project plan. Over time, however, she has become adept at shifting the focus from frustration to setting out the options that work for her in such a way that they move others to action, versus remaining stuck in their uncertainty.

Heather has learned to recognize what she can live with and what aligns with the company priorities, then finding the next best step (or two). This helps shift from the waiting game to managing what's in her control and what must be shifted to someone else's plate. Heather has practiced making decisions at home, work, and with clients. It's not just a business development strategy, but a strategy for life. Being able to make decisions and move forward has allowed a new sense of calm, more time to focus on true priorities, and the ability to act as a guiding force (especially when paired with a two hoots approach).

***

Good decisions are more than options; they are a strategic tool used to move priorities and plans forward. When done right, they build trust. They also demonstrate the depth of your knowledge and care for a client. They are at the center of any business plan and key to knowing where to put yourself in the market.

Your Task List

1. **Pick one night during the week and decide what dinner will be in advance.** Make it something you know you will enjoy and can either pick up or make with ease. Practice announcing "this is what's for dinner!" with enthusiasm and without wavering.

2. **Practice making business decisions and presenting them to yourself as part of your Monthly Meeting.** Pick one goal and focus on narrowing down two options that are feasible. Make a strong decision that is aligned with your energy and goals.

3. **Sharing your expertise is a great way to expand your presence within the market.** Make a big list of all the topics that are interesting to you to share in an article, client alert, or LinkedIn post. Narrow down the options to those most important to your clients. Select two and practice offering them up to either a collaborator or client on what they want to learn more about.

Do Something

The most important part of a business development strategy is taking the first step. Get that done and the rest will follow.

When my grandmother came to live in Kansas City, my days became filled with unexpected doctor's visits and random calls asking my opinion about caregivers and medication—none of which was in my wheelhouse. The unexpected nature of the conversations threw me and my schedule into turmoil. To combat this, I started waking up every morning at five and making soup. The story I told myself was that my kids loved homemade soup in their lunches. In reality, it started my day doing something, which often led to doing other things.

My soup schedule had rules:

1. **No baby carrots.** I needed to peel and dice the carrots each morning.

2. **The dicing was to be done with care.** I have never been one to understand knife skills, but focusing on trying this skill gave me something to strive for.

3. **No recipe.** Requiring me to tap into my creativity and cooking muscles, I had to lead through trial, error, and a whole lot of tasting.

The result? I can save any pot of soup from disaster. I finally learned how to chop a carrot that won't make you choke in soup, and I can make chicken soup about twenty different ways.

Making a pot of soup is a whole lot like building client relationships. The ingredients of a good conversation and client relationship matter. Caring about the basics creates a better foundation. Stretching your creative muscle provides more options in what you see for solutions and ideas for your clients. Most of all, making the pot of soup is getting one thing done and allows you to get a whole lot more done. In addition, when you can put this process into practice for one client and understand how your advisory role resonates best for clients, you can do it for more (or twenty more if that aligns with your goals).

One Action at a Time

Instead of wondering and waiting for the perfect moment to start building client relationships, doing something each day to nurture your network shifts from waiting for the pause in your practice to making this your practice. Kind of like making a pot of soup.

I could have been stuck in the uncertainty of my days and wondering how to build a book and care for my grandma. Yet the way I survived (and eventually thrived) was not over-thinking it; instead, I put myself into action.

The way forward is often being in action (rather than a holding pattern). It's doing the work and navigating what comes next. Said another way, navigating these pivotal points in your practice starts by letting go of overthinking and taking the first step. You need to drop the misconception that success is found only in working with the "right" clients on the "best" projects, or (worse yet) copying the strategies of others that appear successful from the outside. Instead, you need to focus on finding the simplest, most efficient action step and do that. Once you complete this, it's easy to replicate and expand into something more complex, solely as necessary. This is often how my clients start maximizing the results from the easiest of action steps.

Maximum Results

I'm often asked to share my clients' secrets—the secrets of those who have built incredible careers, not just marked by the numbers or the bottom line, but those that are remarkable in the strength of their network and client relationships and are fully living their lives right now. After giving great thought and attention to the markers of these professionals, I find it comes down to six things:

- They have a growth mindset about their expertise and experience that is marked with humility and a desire to constantly stay on the edge of what's next for their industry, niche, or practice.

- Their commitment to clients and community is not just for the big moments, but the everyday moments. They are consistent in their care and concern, and diligent in nurturing their network.

- They don't just know the goals and priorities of their clients, colleagues, and community; they understand them and support the goals without reservation. They believe in cultivating abundant results by lifting others up and speaking up and out loud about the good work they find in others and mention them by name.

- They know what they love about what they do, and they share it with others. The growth and challenge of building a meaningful practice is fun for them.

- They do the work. They don't just talk about change; they put themselves in the driver's seat to make it happen. This isn't about them knowing what to do, but being willing to find the strategy and support they need while stepping off the starting block.

- They train their teams to ensure their clients have a consistent experience. This starts with making sure their teams understand how to engage in robust conversations, listen carefully, and provide advice consistent with their approach and practice reputation.

This insight doesn't happen by sitting around hoping the answers come to them. They do one thing, and then another.

It's something akin to squeezing growth into the cracks of your day.[31] This approach focuses not on overanalyzing and creating beautiful strategic plans, but engaging with the plan and getting it done.

Leaning into a strategy with relationships, conversations, and collaboration in the center creates a ripple effect from the smallest of successes. I wish I could say this in a fancier way: the simplest "pot of soup" to make each day for your practice is to engage in one good conversation each day to keep your perspective fresh, show up when opportunity is looking for you, and simply be smarter because of this engagement.

---

31 Remember the five-minute networking touch point to start your days. A simple action in a small crack of the day.

Just like I made some magical pots of chicken soup, a simple shift in your view from overanalyzing the options to doing something that sets you into action changes everything about what happens next.

Case Study: Finding Success in the Cracks of the Day

Let me introduce you to my client Georgina. Georgina came focused on elevating her reputation in a niche practice. Her work was well respected and sought after, but she was not the one who was talked about. It felt like a constant search to get the respect needed to be put on the steadier work. She wanted independence and control.

We started by getting curious about the depth of her network and breaking down the extensive amount of knowledge sharing and thought leadership efforts that were already in motion. We took note of the dangling threads; the simplest step to start with was to close loose ends. Our sessions focused primarily on the strategic follow-up that moves relationships forward and nurtures opportunity.

Georgina shifted from caring about being picked to building her own practice. She focused more on creating a practice that had a stronger loop of business and relationships that energized her. With this shift in view, the results came in without the constant push and pull hoping it all worked out.

Readjusting her view from what she didn't have to what was already at her fingertips shifted everything. Starting with homing in on the confidence and clarity with which she shared her expertise, Georgina was able to quickly leverage her already robust system of diverse thought leadership (LinkedIn, client alerts, and panel participation) to nurture her relationships with clients and industry players. Rather than waiting for big open spots on her calendar or an empty task list, Georgina started using the smallest amounts of time open in her day between meetings or when taking a break between billable work (those cracks in the day) to touch base, follow up, and nurture her relationships. She sent simple follow-up emails and didn't stop cultivating relationships in the midst of her busy days. She stayed on top of the conversations with emails and client calls, using them as an opportunity to create work, rather than wait for it.

She matched her deep expertise and market knowledge with the relationships that inspire her every day. As a result, her client development is now easy, her relationships abundant, and yeah, the spotlight on her practice and expertise is shining brightly.

Find the Easiest Way to Try

Growth feels uncomfortable because all the signals point to the need for change. Instead of getting stuck in analysis paralysis, putting a few simple steps into action can help move you from understanding it's time to grow to seeing which steps you can take right now.

At this point, there are a couple different views you can test out, to try something versus waiting for opportunity to step into your office:

- **Client conversations.** Look at this week and notice who you know and talk to as part of your daily life right now. This will allow you to start building a stronger practice with the people and work already filling your days. Get curious about who they are, what you know about them, and what you would like to know.

Ask one question that you wouldn't normally pause to ask. This can be as simple as wondering what other projects they are focused on, or institutional priorities they see shifting. The goal isn't to jump in and offer help, but to notice what excites you about the work they describe. Take notes!

- **Colleague connections.** What are your colleagues working on that sounds interesting? Instead of thinking they have all the luck in getting picked for projects, talk to them and learn about how they are building a practice, what they love about the work, and what they want to change. When you can recognize that everyone is facing certain growth points as part of the natural pace of a practice, it takes the mystery and envy out of the equation.

There are two perspectives, one internal and one external. Together, they provide a foundation for ramping up the energy and enthusiasm to figure out how to make the practice you have start showing the results you have dreamed about since your first day on the job.

***

You have aligned your priorities and decided to do something about where you are and how you view the longevity and growth of your practice. Next, you will rethink how you do these simple things to make your choices reap better results. This comes from adding power and intentionality to the game plan. Believe in the possibilities. Let's start making things happen right now.

Your Task List

1. **Make soup.** Without looking at a recipe, gather the ingredients you would put into a pot of soup. Allow yourself to see what strategies and skills you already have by putting together a tasty meal based on quality and creativity. Allow this to be your first step to practice taking control and choosing action rather than overthinking.

2. **Spend one day thinking about where you spend your time and energy.** Notice every time you think about cultivating client relationships or nurturing your network. What do you notice is getting your attention, what work are you leaving on the table, and where do you need to close loose ends?

3. **Look at your task list and pick the very easiest thing to do that will deepen a client relationship.** Do that one thing and notice how it feels to intentionally prioritize a simple task with a bigger client impact.

Train for Better Results

*Peak performance isn't about being all in,
all the time, with all your energy. Instead,
find your peak through consistently paced
practice, doing the next best thing to
reimagine your practice.*

I would never have called myself an athlete. Growing up in the eighties, the only exercise I knew was Jane Fonda workout tapes and long pool days during the summer. It wasn't until law school and a good friend dragging me to the gym for step class and an introduction to a treadmill that working out became more than my daily physical movement by happenstance. I was healthy and strong but playing it safe. I was using the workouts that seemed to work for others and assumed they were enough for me. I was knowledgeable-ish. I had a very middle-of-the-road approach to physical fitness.

Do you know what a middle-of-the-road attitude and approach creates? Middle-of-the-road results.

I became curious about what kind of growth and excellence could be found if I reconsidered that "good enough" plan. Like most lawyers, being "just OK" was never going to be what I was striving for. I had a short introduction to a new trainer's methodology and found pretty great results within a few short weeks. Curious, I contemplated hiring him as a trainer. And I kept thinking about it, for a year.

In truth, I delayed contacting him because I didn't think I was ready. Similar to stories I hear from prospective clients who contemplate working on growing a book of business *(but need to wait until they have their network organized or have tackled the basics on their own first)*, I thought I needed to get stronger and faster on my own before being worthy of the work with him. One simple mindset shift changed this. Instead of preparing to be better, I decided I could simply be my own version of elite, not someone else's. And I could be ready now.

Jumping ahead, I made the call, and the shift to claiming my own excellence happened overnight.[32] Everything changed by leaning into the concepts of consistency and working with someone who had a whole new view from the next level up.[33]

Work Those Opportunities

Shifting my view of working out immediately shined a light on a concept that plays out for those trying to figure out what to do to make a change or grow their practice: start with ramped-up consistency. Notice I don't say do the same thing all the time over and over again and assume it will work enough to get by. Ramped-up consistency boasts two

---

[32] Welcome Ryan Hopkins to this story. Unlike other people mentioned in this book, I am sharing Ryan's name with all of you with his permission and a promise that he will never share my rambling complaints about reverse lunges and hip flexions.

[33] A self-sustaining practice isn't just bigger but is stepping up and accepting that the way you used to do things doesn't work all that well anymore. This new "level" isn't about having more or boasting bigger numbers (unless you want it to), rather it's about stepping up for the next stage of your practice.

things: power behind it to create better results, and strategy to balance out what you do (kind of like making sure you don't have only upper body workouts and ignore your cardio health).

For my work, this meant balancing my workouts to meet the physical stamina of my career. Workshops, firm facilitations, and cultivating interesting networking events are active tasks that often start with 20,000-step days (in heels). This takes the stamina I gained while learning to run at an excruciatingly slow pace to write *After Hello* and putting some mental and physical power behind it. Having spent years studying and working with professionals, there is a distinct mirror in how you treat yourself and build internal muscles and how you are able to show up and use these muscles for others.

There are three big lessons hidden in this shift:

1. Higher quality training creates higher quality results.

2. Starting slightly underprepared is the best time to start.

3. Leveling up doesn't mean starting over. It means moving forward from where you are right now.

The middle-of-the-road approach shows up equally as strong and present in our networking and client relationships. When you gravitate toward relationships that feel accessible, you typically aim lower than where you and your career goals are headed. You choose safer client conversations to keep the relationship a little less risky, rather than engage in discussions with the decision makers. It's playing it safe where you show up, who you talk to, and the relationships you nurture.

Spending all your time trying to push away bad results reaps average results, at best. Allowing yourself to recognize that leaning into the discomfort of things not quite working out, or simply being a crappy day, isn't nearly as uncomfortable as you imagine. Rather than think you need to get past all those before you take on this new role as CEO, it's time to train into these moments, rather than around them (or trying to outrun them).

Just as I moved myself out of the comfort zone in the gym, you can do the same with your network, relationships, and practice goals. It just takes a different kind of training. The evolution of your practice requires you to take on new habits and other daily tasks that are different than the hard work that got you to this point—because what got you here won't get you there.

- Rather than checking in with partners to see what they need, you are checking in with clients.

- Instead of jumping into action, you are proactively planning ahead to make sure your team resources are allocated to the priorities that matter most, right now.

- Instead of showing up at a conference to be a part of the team, you are setting a client nurturing strategy (at the conference and beyond) into action that is authentic and personalized, while being paced appropriately to keep you top of mind.

These little actions are new muscles that need training. Just like the big changes for your body don't happen by working out at an extreme level all day, every day, neither does stepping up your client development game. It is about consistently getting out of your comfort zone and allowing a whole new foundation to be set for your self-sustaining practice.

Get Better Data

I used to think I was fancy, remembering my heart rate monitor. I tracked workout minutes and closed the rings on a workout to not let my training partners down. Yet none of that data really meant anything to me. Finding better tools (yup, that's the point), Coach Ryan introduced me to a daily plan of understanding not just my heart rate and aerobic goals, but how my nervous system was influencing my energy and output potential (both at work and in the gym).

We started focusing on peak performance for where I am each day. While the data was simple to compile each day (about three minutes), the information had to feel significant enough in its results to give me the incentive to keep tracking it. The detailed information changed my view of how data could influence and impact my performance in all aspects of my workouts, work, and life.

What does this look like for business development? When it comes to building a better-quality practice, where you put your energy and focus matters.

The safe version: stay in the supporting role and let others be the ones leading the pitches, client development planning, and focus on building friendships hoping they look to you for help one day. Waiting is safe. It is also safe to always want to work with the beginners. The more experienced your clients, the higher their expectations.

The reach version: Allow yourself to recognize the vast contacts and connections you have built up over the years. Some may have gone quiet or become not "as close," but the starting point is already in motion. Put yourself into uncomfortable positions, situations where you get to meet and know the clients you want to work with: raise your hand for panels, co-author articles, gather interesting clients to get to know each other, or be the planner for the conference party. And when you make it happen, say "yes" when someone hands you the microphone to welcome others. Allow yourself to be known and get to know the people who are interested in you and your expertise.

One Cautionary Tip

Try to avoid the instinct to go "all in" and leave no energy or stone unturned in case there is opportunity to be had. This means doing anything and everything you can to the point of almost being overbearing. Combined with high client demands for responsiveness, this approach is a recipe for burnout. This all-or-nothing attitude never allows you to gain momentum or test the results of any business development strategy, leading to flawed data and shaky results. Once a break happens, so does the crash of energy and effort. As a business development and practice growth strategy, this is flawed in approach and execution.

Rather than do everything and then nothing, ramp up your consistency as you identify the strategy that works best for you. Consistently engage in building your network and nurturing the relationships you want to grow. When paced appropriately, your networking and business development muscles strengthen, and the outcomes become more apparent.

While your data collection in the past has been centered around your billable hours in a day and originations for the year, might I offer a few different metrics to focus on—not only to understand your everyday successes, but what you can do with the potential and energy you have available[34]:

1. **Start with self-care.** Wellness initiatives have been kept out of the equation for too long, and in fact directly impact your ability to engage with others, spot issues, and think clearly. Pick one metric (sleep, hydration, movement) and track it over a month. Not necessarily to change anything, but to notice how it influences your energy and capacity for "more" when it is in a healthier state.

2. **Count the conversations.** Sometimes a number game comes into play. Without growing your network and engaging with your connections, you are simply gathering new contact info to add to your email directory. How many conversations with clients (current and potential), colleagues, or referral partners have you had this month? Keep a tally sheet by, or on, your phone. These numbers tell a story and help guide the next strategic decision of where to focus your efforts.

3. **Connection score.** Since you aren't just looking to build a big list of connections and contacts, you need to understand how well you are nurturing mutually connected relationships. Consider your closest relationships and those you want to nurture. How connected do you feel to these individuals? Look at what you know about their current priorities, plans,

---

34 Just in case you aren't spotting the trend, the focus here is on doing something. What you do and have capacity for is not based on what client work you have right now but on what options and choices you create from everyday actions. You are putting your desire to move through a growth point into action.

and stress points. How well are you nurturing those relationships and, in turn, allowing yourself to share your goals and priorities? Consider giving this a numerical rating so you can track this data over time.

If you jump ahead to the task list, these three metrics are great ones to consider for your Monthly Meeting. They also allow you to embody and embrace better training for better results, allowing you to simply get started.

Now, there is an uneasiness in this structured approach. It forces you to organize your thoughts, to note what works and what doesn't work. As such, some may feel it somehow negates the authenticity of your efforts. But allowing yourself the support of reminders amid your busy days decreases the chance of business development taking the back seat, or worse, waiting until you have the free time.

Start Before You Are Ready

Remember how I waited to level up my strength strategy until I was ready? Well, a year of waiting didn't move the needle in terms of readiness. It turns out raising your hand to change your strategy now is a whole lot better than waiting for your preparation and readiness to perfectly line up. Because it rarely happens. In the waiting game, you never think it's quite your turn. This is reinforced by the fear of failure or harsh criticism for taking on a growth step that is a possible misstep.[35]

---

35 Jahna Berry shares insights on how to get past these hurdles in the *Harvard Business Review* article, "Why You Should Take on More Stretch Assignments," including the tip to use a listening tour to gain confidence in the next step and stretch assignment. Check it out: https://hbr.org/2023/04/why-you-should-take-on-more-stretch-assignments.

Deepening a client relationship (or taking the risk of starting a new one) often feels like a stretch you might not be ready for or could cause you to fall on your face. So, you wait. You convince everyone, including yourself, that there just isn't the bandwidth to take on the work. *You probably won't be picked; it probably won't work out. It likely won't give you the traction you need to get past this pivot point.*

This mindset is a combination of the two kinds of readiness: physical and mental.

The physical readiness in client development is having the time, financial resources, and energy to focus on the tasks at hand. Given the very nature of your practice, free time and space are rarely noticeable enough to make you feel ready and available to commit to what seems should be a massive commitment. Stop waiting for this feeling. Instead, fit in what you can to keep the ball rolling. Focus on momentum rather than monumental business development plans. As discussed in the last chapter, finding the cracks in your day to get things done shifts you into action and offers the opportunity to make more changes as you need to.

The trick is to keep the tasks that allow you to stay consistent extremely simple. To get you started, here are a few five-minute investments—choosing one a day is sufficient to consistently nurture your network, client relationships, and potential new business:

- Get in the habit of quick (three to five sentence) emails to touch base and check in on clients and further your last conversation. It's much easier than mapping out a client nurturing sequence of six emails and glossy newsletters.

- Use the beginning or end of project calls to get insight and input from clients, looping them into your business development plans from the start. There's no need for a webinar and panel discussion before you know clients are interested in and engaged in the topic.

- Follow up on new client introductions to make sure they don't have any open questions. A short email should suffice.

- Share a good article you wrote, or think is relevant, to a potential client to get their input and further your focus on the topic.

Note: None of these options cost you more than a few minutes. Let's dispel the myth that big budgets and large blocks of time are required for the self-sustaining practice you are looking for. While I am absolutely not suggesting the elimination of client development budgets, they are not a requirement at this stage.

Rather than provide a laundry list of ideas for five-minute connections,[36] the point is that a five-minute connection is worth more in the long run than waiting to clear the desk, open your calendar, align the best colleagues, and plan something spectacular. While I'm not opposed to a well-executed strategy, the little details that five-minute tasks take care of are often more noticed and appreciated than the big invitation that isn't relevant enough to wow the client.

The simple part is slipping those strategic tools and touchpoints into your days. The harder part is allowing yourself to

---

36 Want a quick way to get started? You'll find is a list that will jumpstart these conversations in *Know Your Clients*, available at https://debfeder.com/clients.

do this without knowing what ready feels like and trusting that you can do this. The mental ready point often feels like the hunt for a fresh start. It's important to build the ability to shift and grow and figure things out while still managing your practice.

Not thinking you are ready can't be ignored, nor just pushed away. Instead, you've got to prove to yourself you are ready enough. You don't learn calculus in kindergarten or start benching 100 pounds in the gym on day one. Similarly, you don't need to go overboard expanding your practice from the start. You also don't need to be ready to manage a ten-million-dollar book before starting a meaningful focus on business development.[37]

Pick one client to focus on with whom you would like to expand the work you do for them, and possibly cross-sell other professionals within your firm:

1. Spend five minutes brainstorming what you know, and the alignment points you can see with all the practices you can think of (and maybe learn about by talking to colleagues).

2. Spend five minutes talking with them this week on what their big priorities are and setting up a time to dive into this a bit further when you both have time in the next few weeks.

3. Keep a brainstorm sheet for this one client and this one focused idea to jot down notes of ways to share

---

37 Here's what I tell every client who shares this concern: "Don't walk away from the opportunity because you are scared to manage that. I will help you put the plans in place and find the help, but never let that keep you from raising your hand and building the self-sustaining practice you are looking for."

your expertise, whom to introduce, and where each of these ideas align with the client's priorities and goals.

And just like that, over the span of a week, you've had a client conversation. You've shifted your view from *this is all my strategy* to involving others; from focusing on going after work to getting strategic in aligning what you do and what they need. Not bad and not too much too soon such that it overwhelms what you've already committed to.

A Reboot Doesn't Mean You Start Over

I love a fresh start. Whether it's a new planner or new workout plan, I love the feeling of a clean slate and the opportunity to get it right. While this seems enticing, it's often a fool's errand to think you get a fresh start like this when your practice is already in motion. Instead of looking to do things over, focus on hitting the reboot button.

While writing this book, I went to Coach Ryan and asked for a reboot. Coming off family vacation and needing some fresh energy for the final push to get this book done, I was ready to change up my workouts and push the limits a bit. But I also wanted a clean slate to start from. The very first message I got was, "This is great, but a reboot doesn't mean a restart. It just means we change things up from where you are today."

The reboot worked and changed my view of my goals. It can do the same for you. A reboot will allow you to take stock of where you are today, what muscles, habits, or strategies need focus, and what moving the goal line right now could look like. This simple analysis gets you started, rather than moving back to the beginning and hoping you get it right. Ultimately, it allows you to build the stronger habits and work muscles needed to show up for your clients with consistency, clarity, and confidence.

Consistency Is the Game Changer

When it comes to relationships that have the most influence on your career, consistency is key—particularly when you consider how you want to build your network, nurture relationships, and share your expertise. We'll discuss the mechanics of these consistent choices later, but for now let's dispel the myth and set the standards for "consistent".

Being consistent doesn't mean: doing everything, all the time, every day.

Being consistent does mean:

- **Growing your network** of relationships by setting up a consistent plan to be welcoming and interested in new connections (or reconnecting with those who you lost touch with but want to be part of your circle).

- **Nurturing current relationships** by showing up more than occasionally, staying in the conversation, and being a consistent option as a work resource.

- **Sharing your expertise** in a meaningful way throughout the year so all your hard work and experiences are shared with more than just your mom on the drive home from work.

- **Finding the rhythm and pacing** that works for your practice and goals. If you need a big reboot, the numbers and frequency need to adjust. If you are buried and at capacity, you need to know how to slow the pace without dropping off the radar altogether.

With these consistent shifts, you will get better data that provides a more complete picture to the originations, collections, and billable hours you currently track. Instead of focusing on the high-level numbers, you need to align your focus to the size and strength of your network, as well as the quality, pace, and results from more meaningful conversations.

Case Study: Steady Does Win the Race

Meet my client, Claire, a big law partner who was sitting at a growth point. She knew she needed to dramatically shift how she practiced and was resetting her practice with a new team. That meant starting over with her book of business.

Instead of planning a big strategy, we focused on setting up micro-networking goals and conversation strategies for each month, month after month. The feedback was great, but business was slow to come in. A few points along the way, we had to double down on staying steady and patient in the midst of waiting for clients to need her professional services. Claire focused on building layers to her network, both internally and externally. Her long-standing connections became stronger. Her willingness to expand her network became bolder. There was an unwavering commitment to the process, rather than grasping for results. Claire understood the power in consistently executing with confidence and care.

What happened? Claire's book didn't just grow, it exploded. Her team grew and her relationships and reputation strengthened. Today, she is not only the one to call for this work, but a rising star in supporting the practices of so many others. She is generous with collaborations and always willing to go the extra mile for clients—and she's having a whole lot of fun along the way. All because Claire stayed steady, consistent, and didn't let the worry of what might happen change the strategy along the way.

Boldly expanding your network requires grabbing those binoculars and flashlight we talked about earlier. Stop looking at your work with a limited view and recognize who you know and what connections match the work you want to do now and tomorrow (not what you used to do ten years ago). Bold doesn't mean brash (or pushy), but it does mean picking up the phone and talking to the person you met at the conference. It does mean following up with an old colleague who has landed the dream job (and happens to be a dream client for you). It does mean making friends with the senior people on your own team, and client teams. And it does mean refusing to go back to crisis mode when things aren't moving in the direction you want them to, as quickly as you'd like. Trust the process; be consistent in your small, forward-moving steps.

***

When it comes to training your physical body, recovery is just as important as the workout itself. Proper rest, hydration, and nutrition help your muscles heal and help make you stronger. Recovery is important when building your career, as well. You want to work smarter, not harder. When you balance your choices to allow for consistency in the work, it allows for rest, which is a game changer. Rest allows you to be mindful in your approach and put a training plan into action. It allows you to coach yourself through the hard bits, by giving you the time and resources to remember your progress. It allows you to see the bigger picture and move into bigger, bolder, stronger conversations and connections—and enjoy the journey along the way.

Your Task List

1. **Using the monthly meeting agenda you created, add more detail based on three metrics from this chapter that hold the most meaning to you right now.** Give yourself a score of 1–5 (one is low, five is high) each month, for each metric and identify one opportunity to shift in the coming month.

2. **Remember the client you would replicate if you could?** Pick one client that most closely resembles this work and reach out for a conversation. Learn what they care about and practice engaging in conversations with those who energize and excite you.

3. **Make a rest and recharge plan.** This can be added to your monthly meeting, it can be found on the #BizDeb Monthly Calendar,[38] or you can make your own plan. Pick at least three things that help you rest (other than shutting down and leaving the office for ten days). They need to be microbreaks, something that can happen right in the middle of a busy day and allow you to reset amidst chaos. Make a plan to test each over the next week.

---

38 The #BizDeb Calendar evolved to create the consistency plan for those cracks in the day. If you want to take a look, send hello@debfeder.com a message and ask for a Calendar Pass.

Keep Your Attention on Your Whole Network

There are three distinct parts to cultivating client relationships that bring in business: building a network, engaging with your network, and sharing what you do with confidence and clarity.

Years ago, I was sitting at a conference room table as part of a team when I got pulled off to tackle an emergency project that had a courier arriving within the hour to pick up the papers. No time to move our unnecessarily large laptops and network cables, I quickly asked the room if I could just focus for one hour while I raced against the clock. Throwing my earplugs in, I did my best to start chipping away at the last details. Above the din of my classical music (trying to stay calm), I could hear a woman at the table start to sing over and over again, *"Every party has a pooper, and in this room, it's Deb."* Trying my best to ignore this woman, a friend of mine across the table (let's call her Charlotte) spent her energy keeping me focused, sending me funny notes and making sure my attention was spent on the project, and not the childish tirade. The punchline: the singer (as we will call her) didn't stick around much longer, while Charlotte and I are still close and have celebrated being in each other's lives for more than two decades. We have celebrated our children's milestones together, talked late into the night while caring for ailing relatives, and worked through the massive grief of burying family members. More than anything, we have each other's backs in both business and life, spot opportunities the other might be interested in, and celebrate all our accomplishments (big and small).

As this friendship illustrates, a pillar of a healthy career is quality relationships. These relationships are with other very smart, motivated individuals who are willing to work together, jump in as needed, give wise and balanced advice, and generously share work as appropriate. Most of all, they are with people who care.

The Nurture Zone

You have a lot of contacts in your phone and email directory. You have plenty of followers on social media, and you know people when you go places. That means your network is strong, right? Not necessarily.

It just means you have a lot of names in the buckets of your life. Without nurturing these connections (starting with a simple *Hello* and expanding to get to know them), it's simply contact information.

Once connections are made, they should be firmly placed in the Nurture Zone. In other words, they are in a place where you keep in touch and continue learning about them. There are many ways to go about this; here are a few ideas to start with:

1. Check in.
2. Share an article.

3. Make an introduction.
4. Follow up on that idea.
5. Invite them to something.
6. Continue the conversation.
7. Meet up for lunch, coffee, or a walk.
8. Reconnect if it's been a while.

You get the point. These connections are all moving along in your Nurture Zone, and when paced correctly, you are touching base with each of them in appropriate intervals (not some robotic schedule, or worse, robotic form email produced by an app, but by judging the conversation and mutual interests of both small talk and professional relationships). You are also setting reminders to not forget the follow up that allows you to carry the conversation forward.

From time to time, you pause the movement of all those within the Nurture Zone by sharing your expertise in a way that everyone can hear and take it in. This happens in the form of a LinkedIn post, client alert, webinar, or podcast (just to name a few outlets that are most common). At this point the content loops back into your conversations and adds a new layer to engage your relationships in a way that doesn't just shout: "Hi, I am an expert!" Instead, it allows you to learn from your connections: how they see similar hot topics, what interests them about it, or what they want someone else to take care of.

Notice how the work comes from the spaces in each of these engagements. It happens more by paying attention and being authentic within the interaction with your network far more often than a big, bold impromptu pitch that wasn't invited from the get-go.

A Thought About Social Media Interactions

When talking to new clients about how they currently nurture connections within their network, I often hear about their interactions on LinkedIn and Instagram. While this is a way to support a connection and recognize their expertise, it is not automatically a nurture point that progresses your relationship or conversations forward. Hitting "like" on a post doesn't provide the personal connection that expands conversations. What it can do, when done well, is allow you to send a separate note to talk about the post, update, or milestone they are celebrating. This is when social media and your networking strategy work well together.

Nurturing Builds a Strong Foundation

Take my friendship with Charlotte. Our relationship started with daily interaction, by assignment rather than by choice or design. Using this opportunity to get to know each other, our trust evolved day after day. That built a solid foundation. Even when life separated us by priorities and obligations, trust remained.

It makes engaging with each other (from a space of a more dormant connection) as easy as sending a text with a random question. We can hopscotch right over the niceties of "what have you been up to" and ask whether they have ever heard of (insert name of professional connection, hot new restaurant, or random internet fact).

You might think we have talked each week for the better part of twenty years. Nope. Not even close. In fact, there have been a few years in there where we have texted or grabbed coffee once or twice, but the foundation of our relationship has sustained us. With kids now grown, and new priorities, we see each other often and can trust the sounding board on the other end of the line.

Building a self-sustaining practice asks you to lean in and not just rely on these relationships, but nurture and grow them with the same tenacity as when you launched your career.

The importance of professional friendships comes not just from supportive colleagues, but from clients as well. As your career matures, the people around you play a significant part in your day (and life), and cultivating healthy working relationships goes a long way not only in managing your days but strengthening your career and book of business.

Consider the Trajectory of a Strong, Professional Relationship

You meet someone at a conference. Let's call her Simone. You had a great connection with her talking all about a mutual college connection and briefly talked about the work you each do. Returning to the office, you have a few options:

1. Hope Simone reaches out to you. This is how you will know if you read the situation correctly.

2. Send Simone a LinkedIn connection request with a note saying, "Nice to meet you at the conference."

3. Follow up with an article that mentions your alma

mater and the late-night eats on campus. Not able to resist continuing the conversation that you started about the turkey sandwich that was your late-night food of choice, you send it over and ask which of the spots Simone has tried.

Choosing Option 3 moves Simone from "someone you met" into an active connection and a relationship that is ready for you to engage with as part of your network. Now, most people think one or two things will happen with Simone:

- One, your initial instincts were a bit off. Her budget, priorities, and work don't really align for you and so you consider her a nice person you met at a conference and push the relationship out of your network with the label: not worth it.

- Or, two, Simone is your dream client. She has an active project waiting for you and is happy to sign your engagement agreement today. Her company values high-level expertise and pays your A-rates without flinching, while simultaneously telling you that they never work past five, the projects are not urgent, and she prefers to connect after yoga. Simone isn't just a great client; she is your new BFF!

The reality is that neither of these options is the most likely one to develop in that instant. Most relationships that you move into the Nurture Zone are doing just that: moving in and engaging with you in this space for days, weeks, and often years. What happens while they are in the Nurture Zone determines whether or not that simple *Hello* and casual conversation turn into a relationship—either as a colleague, friend, referral partner, or client.

Keep Your Network Active

The common theme here is simple. Your life is filled with people. These people are part of a virtual contact list (or real one if you've gone to the trouble) that are waiting for engagement. When you reach out and say *Hello* in any capacity, you move them into the active part of your network. Keeping in touch and pacing conversations to build trust and a mutual respect for who each of you are and what you do nurtures the relationship. Finally, sharing your expertise from time to time is a relationship enhancer.

Now, there is a lingering question regarding how much of this can be outsourced to administrative teams, marketing or business development teams, or AI. While you might be able to set up schedules that monitor your touchpoints with the active members of your network, most of this work is on you. Why? Because higher-level relationships require the intuitive understanding of not just the position of your connection, but the base of your human connection (those common points that launched the conversation or introduction in the first place)—and those working at the top of their field can judge this a mile away. This human connection also knows the appropriate information and approach for a personalized strategy.

Let's put this into action for you.

Pick someone you work with who you would like to build a stronger, more collaborative relationship with (you want to be picked as part of their next big team, you see mutual opportunity for client services, or you want them to be hollering your name all over the firm as the one to know).

Next, consider when you have done the following:

1. Reached out and said *Hello* other than in passing at a practice group meeting or the annual partner meeting.

2. Shared your specific expertise or interest in exploring more about their practice (more than merely asking, "What are you working on these days?").

3. Introduced them to someone else at the firm.

4. Forwarded an article or content update you think they would find interesting.

5. Learned about their life outside of the firm (and remembered their kids' names for once).

Each of these is an opening that allows your relationship to settle before you throw out the collaboration plan you have been hatching in the back of your brain ever since you were a summer associate.

Next, consider what information could be helpful to anyone within the firm who could support your practice, and is the expertise clients are actively seeking (or should be) right now. Make a list of what you see as potential content to start cultivating.

Great! You now have a series of conversations that can be paced over time. You have ideas on information that's worth sharing, as well as context around what you need to learn about the senior partner's practice. You have a solid follow-up plan that will allow you to authentically spread your expertise and practice—to be both helpful and let more people know about this area of interest.

Now, if you were to make this level of detailed notes for everyone in your network, it would be an unwieldy task requiring too much time that you don't have. It's also unnecessary. As a launch point, you start with those in your inner circles and notice what works best for your own pacing, workspace, and approach. Finding some latitude to test and tweak the emails and touchpoint conversations, you can easily implement this nurturing strategy without overwhelming your calendar or energy.

Case Study: Reconnection Creates Opportunity

Meet my client, Avery. Avery came to me with a successful big law litigation practice. Since she knew how to grow her business, her focus was being able to rely on a business development strategy that sustained her current success and allowed her to narrow the work to match her unique skillset in the industry.

Diving into her networking strategy, it quickly became apparent that it was a big network without a consistent nurturing plan. In addition, many of Avery's contacts were older connections that hadn't been spoken to and there was opportunity sitting in her contact list. Avery set up a plan to work through the contact list, one page at a time. She didn't just look up names and emails but reached out and used it as an opportunity to reconnect with those on her list, refresh the conversation, and reboot quiet relationships. Avery used a getting organized task to her business development advantage. She added a new level of energy into her network simply by committing to making sure she had the right contacts and details in a place that worked for her.

Don't Overlook Potential

A Potential is someone you know, have been introduced to, or used to know at some point. You don't know much about them other than what you can find from a quick modern-day cyber-stalking session. They might remember you, or they might not. But you have a name and that makes you one step closer to getting them into your network and building a relationship.

Once you reach out and talk to this Potential, you have moved them from a passive connection into an active relationship. But don't be deceived. Many mistake this first *Hello* and engagement as a tight-knit relationship in the making. Instead, it's a relationship for you to nurture—a chance for them to get to know you and you to learn and cultivate a relationship with them.

Make Way for Glimmers of Possibility

Rather than spend energy worrying if hard times will happen to you, know they will. The instinct in these moments is to start picking apart what is on your desk and thinking through all clients you know to try and find the hidden work. As we've discussed, the invitation is to stop staring at the problem and focus on engaging with your network to widen your view and shift your mood.

One conversation with a client, colleague, family member, or friend can change everything. Reach out to your network for a simple conversation. Not to focus on what's wrong or your worries (at least not at first) but to reconnect and recognize what everyone else is focused on around you. The very nature of a thriving practice often means your focus is narrowed to the point where you cannot see the distance. That one phone call or email is the equivalent of grabbing binoculars and recognizing that you have a whole new view to consider in front of you.

These glimmers are due in large part to a strong network. Bumps are inevitable, yet the stronger the network, the easier the bounce back to get you into the game and engaged in the work. That's why it's best not to wait until you need your network to consider growing and strengthening these relationships. Building a consistent plan to continuously nurture your current relationships, as well as engage new ones, makes work opportunities and support a whole lot easier to find when you are ready (or when it's a necessity).

Consider what it feels like to get that cold call from an old friend who needs you to make an introduction. You feel used and a bit put out. They haven't bothered to reach out for your life milestones, or to even say *Hello*. How galling to think you would use your network to make a strong ask for someone you haven't talked to in twenty years!

But what if they had checked in from time to time, asked about your family and work, sent you an article that reminded you of the old days, or posted a reunion picture that made you laugh and know you missed out on the fun? Now, that call asking you to engage isn't out of the blue. It doesn't seem hard. You knew them back then, and you know them now.

***

The goal isn't to spend all day every day nurturing your network. You want to implement a simple strategy that allows you to cultivate a thriving network in just a few minutes a day. It allows you to spot strong connections and strengthen ones that have somehow gotten lost through life. This network, and the relationships that come from it, are the key to turning those bumps into glimmers. This happens one conversation at a time.

Your Task List

1. **Pick three friends, colleagues, or clients that you enjoy.** Send them each an email to connect and sit down for a good conversation. No need to make this about anything other than catching up. Notice how your mood shifts and the ideas that are sparked from these simple conversations.

2. **Make a list of three clients you would like to get to know better.** Gather your research about the company and industry. The goal is not to sound super smart, but enter the conversation confident, prepared, and interested. If you are ready, reach out and set up a time to connect and learn about their current priorities and projects. This isn't about pitching but about deepening your understanding of them and the work they care about right now.

3. **Take a look at the list under The Nurture Zone.** Identify which of those nurturing activities seem reasonable, which feel challenging, and which you would never do no matter how much I begged. Add your own two or three nurture ideas to the list to start building your go-to file for keeping connections and conversations warm by nurturing your network.

The Continuous Growth of Your Network

Your network is the gas behind your business development strategy. Keep the tank full.

As soon as I moved to Kansas City in early 2000, other than passing the bar, my only other goal was to meet people. Trying to adjust to a new town, I welcomed introductions from family friends and vividly remember an interaction with someone I hoped might be a new friend (or even friendly acquaintance). We had a great first call. Kind of the equivalent to a blind date, easy banter revealed we shared mutual interests, connections, and approach to twenty-something social lives. At the end of the call when normally you say, "Let's get together," she said, "You seem great, but my friends and I aren't taking any new friend applications right now."

I can't make this up.

While the conversation stung and I momentarily wondered if all potential friends were going to be as unwelcoming as this, I was struck by the utter audacity that someone would cut off their network from growth, certain that they knew everyone they would ever want or need to know.

A short-sighted view at best, this attitude and approach is working without the wider and longer-range view your binoculars provide.

Don't Limit Your Network

There are a variety of reasons why you never want to stop growing your network: the people around you change as your practice matures; life happens, and you need connections or introductions to new resources, new cities, or new ideas; you're simply ready to expand your circle of friends, colleagues, and community. And yeah, you want to bring in more business.

Yet, it's far too easy to look at your contacts and feel your network is expansive enough. Maybe you're really comfortable with current friends and connections. Or maybe you feel unable to keep up as it is. *I don't need to add anyone to my network, until someone is worth the pursuit.*

Sounds a whole lot like the woman not taking applications. (I wonder if things would have been different if I was seen as an "influencer" of today—or if she knew she would get something out of the friendship?)

Client development and new business is an obvious goal of any thriving practice, but when your network growth strategy is built off chasing clients, you are keeping it transactional. Shifting away from seeking the relationships that are worth it, you broaden your scope of connections and the resulting conversations. You just might be surprised by what happens next.

For example, years ago, I received a strategy call intake form; I read it, shrugged my shoulders, and wondered how to carefully connect this potential client with a better resource that was aligned with his practice and goals. From what I read in the intake notes and from a quick search online, I didn't feel all that aligned. That being said, I joined the call ready to learn enough to make sure my instincts about who to introduce him to were correct. Except he started the call with, "I couldn't put this into the intake, but I am set to take over my firm and want to hire you to coach me and train my entire senior team to start thinking about business development and how we use LinkedIn differently."

Yeah, that is directly in my line of work and wasn't just a little project but a great client relationship that launched from that moment. If I had brushed off the strategy call from my limited outside knowledge, I would never have had that work. I would have also sent out into the world the reputational note that I am not the one to call for business development reboots. This would be directly contrary to what I want others to know about me and my work. By taking the call and staying open, the work aligned itself.

The lesson: There's magic in leaning in to meet new people, learn from different perspectives, and widen your view of potential from people you have never met.

It's Not a Numbers Game

One important caveat before you get started growing your network. This isn't about adding names to your CRM or new connections on LinkedIn or Instagram, just for the sake of adding numbers. It's also not about going out and meeting as many people as possible for the sake of saying you have grown your network.

For all practical purposes, getting a bunch of names added to any list is just new names being added to a list. (You may recall from the last chapter, these are Potentials.)

You need to shift your view of what a network looks like. Then you can focus on where you are growing and align new connections with this updated perspective. The key is to be thoughtful and deliberate about expanding the circle of the Nurture Zone on a consistent basis, allowing new connections, conversations, and work to naturally grow from your efforts.

Your Network Needs Layers

There are four trees in our yard that were planted when our house was built in the early 1960s. If you look closer, you can see the next grouping of trees that were planted shortly after that. If you keep looking, you can create a timeline of the house and ownership by the trees and choices in landscaping. There are layers to the trees, and their growth tells a story.

Similarly, you want your network layers to tell a story. You have your connections from school and those first few years of a job. You have clients and colleagues from the stage when you first started taking the lead on projects. You have friends and connections from your family obligations and community involvement. You might have moved and made new connections along the way. Each of these individuals provides layers to your network. Some of them grow distant, while others stay steady and grow over time.

The goal is to continue your network growth strategy to allow the layers to naturally prune themselves and regenerate ideas, collaborations, and client relationships.

Said another way, if your network is tight and small, without growth, you will eventually work through all the opportunities within your own sphere and be left expecting your practice growth to happen from the efforts of someone else's networking plan. My suggestion? Have your own strategy that supports you and your team. In turn, you can grow mutually collaborative opportunities through the connections and efforts found in aligning networking strategies with professionals within your now expanded sphere.

Here's an example: if you look at one slice of my network, you will find lots of professionals in private practice. One of these professionals, Laura (yup, from *Tell Me More*), has more industry connections in her niche. Laura and I like to host dinner parties whenever I am in town, to bring together members of our respective networks. This creates new conversations and introduces others who need to know each other. Through these intentional networking moments, I introduced a former boss's daughter to industry connections for a professional move she was wanting to make, and introduced my best friend from college to new connections in the city she was moving to. My college friends happen to send their kids to camp with the kids of a colleague of Laura's, so everyone already knew each other. Out of these dinners there have been new transactions, professional relationships launched, and friendships made.

Now, with a diverse group of professional women, what do we possibly have to talk about? There are three conversations that come up every time:

1. **The University of Michigan and college late-night eats.** This is also one of my favorite small talk conversations to help people learn to enjoy the lighter banter they have forever tried to avoid.

2. **Needlepoint.** Laura has created an unprecedented following of people trying a new hobby based solely off her enthusiasm for her passion. It has shaped activities at #BizDeb retreats, and an endless number of people are fascinated with giving it a try (including me).

3. **Great dinner parties.** What you like in them, what you don't. Where you want to go eat and what makes a good dinner a great one.

Notice that these topics aren't obsessing about driving business conversations. Nor do they force someone to enter someone else's network. Yet the casual nature of conversation and intentional gathering combine to create a ripe environment for finding mutual casual interests and alignment of business interests.

The results of the networking aren't static. Once they are in motion, the opportunities continue to flow as long as you nurture the new connection. What does nurturing your network look like when you are focused on building it and keeping it strong?

- It looks like touching base with someone you just met and expressing interest in continuing the conversation.

- It means making intentional connections and introductions between members of your network who might benefit from knowing each other.

- It means caring about the stuff other people share and staying interested in it (or at least remembering enough to spot stuff that they might enjoy as it comes across your radar).

- It means checking in and caring about the connections you have—and investing in the relationship more often than just when you need something from them.

One note: While a network is important to growing your book, if you keep this shallow perspective, others will feel that intention and respond accordingly. All that means is that if you plan on having fake relationships that are sales-y and surface-level just for the sake of practice metrics, everyone can see it, and it doesn't do anything to help grow trusted relationships that deepen your professional presence and build a self-sustaining practice.

Get Intentional with Growing Your Network

Now that we've established the necessity of growing a network, it's time to get real about growing it. This was easier in middle school, where you could expand your network by simply going and sitting at a different table in the lunchroom. As a grown-up, in an ever-disconnected professional world, you have to go find people:

- **Conferences.** Not to be obvious, but professional gatherings provide a great opportunity to expand your network. There is a common bond already in place. Be selective about which ones you take the time for; focus on those that have people you want to connect and hang out with.

- **Hobbies.** It might not be needlepoint, but hanging out with others who like what you do creates an instant connection. Running clubs, pickleball, and gaming are just a few hobbies that I hear about all the time from clients and my network.

- **Your neighborhood.** When was the last time you took a walk and said *Hello* to the people who live around you? Invite a few neighbors to invite a few neighbors and instantly you have plans on a Saturday night and are meeting new people.

- **Professional networks.** This might be industry groups or retreats. It could be a coaching cohort or alumni club. There is a plethora of options to find professionals and expand who you know.

Don't overthink the groups to join, but find one and dive in. Get involved and see if the people you meet enrich your network and motivate you to commit more time or energy to these commitments. If the answer is no, try something new.

***

While it's vital you nurture the network you have, it is also essential to continue expanding your circle. This expansion allows for new ideas and approaches to influence your work. It allows you to mature in ways you couldn't have seen from the prior pivot point, and it allows you to capitalize on the right options for you and your practice. Rather than shutting off a new friendship because your life and community feel full, be open to what happens when you generously invite someone else into your circle.

Your Task List

1. **Make a list of people you have met over the last few months.** How many of these new connections have you touched base with since your initial meeting? Remember to reach out and make an effort to extend the connection with a call, email, or invitation.

2. **If you had to describe your network in words rather than numbers, how would you describe it?** How would you like to describe it? Where is the gap in these descriptions?

3. **Draw out the layers of your network.** Do you spend more time with older connections or those you've met more recently? Do you nurture one group over another? Think about which layer needs growth and strengthening. Once you notice it, you can align your networking choices to fill in your network accordingly.

Practice Radical Generosity

A self-sustaining practice isn't built by grabbing everything for yourself but embodying an abundance mindset that permeates everything you do.

There is something about having a family member get significantly sick that brings a new level of humanity to the forefront. Meal trains, kid carpools, laundry, you name it. It is really easy to snap into action when someone you love is hurting. My friends sort of shoved me into accepting help when taking care of my mom (and again with my grandmother). My kids were somehow scooped up and invited everywhere, including a campsite set up in a friend's house to make it feel like an adventure. My floors were swept and dishes washed when I just didn't have one more ounce of energy. These friends were modeling what generosity looks like, and how good it can be to accept it.

But there is a little secret in the world of those of us who've gone through it: the meals will end. The wisdom is, "Show up later, because the meals will stop and someone might need something down the road." You see, people stop coming around within days after a funeral or when the illness seems under control. The generosity ends.

That's why consistent generosity makes you stand out from the crowd. And why it's essential in building the practice you want and can be proud of.

Build a Practice of Everyday Generosity

What if you show up to help someone whose workload is burying them, or offer an idea to the client who simply needs someone to talk out the problems? What if you got excited (yeah, enthusiasm is a way of expressing generosity) for the big, bold idea of a client or colleague, or took care of the cupcakes when the class mom just doesn't have the bandwidth?

When given in the true spirit of helping others (rather than simply trying to look impressively kind for the sake of client development), it's an expression of character and how you work. If a client thinks that listening to them is just a charitable act, rather than one of true interest, they will be less likely to consider you the trusted thinking partner and advisor they want and need. Yet, if you are not only a great listener but also share your ideas that could help them out because you can't stop thinking about it, they witness your investment in them and their work's prosperity.

For me, one of these ways is nerding out with people about content. Whether it is a LinkedIn post or a keynote, I somehow have become known for my ideas. For example, a client was sharing a travel story, and I was jumping out of my skin, quickly jotting down a keynote that naturally flowed from the story, weaving in their exact practice area and an incredible lesson. In contrast, I have a former client who loves to share family vignettes and weave them into the law. This sparked my imagination when reading an article about a hot topic in their practice; one word was used so much, it annoyed me. The family stories and annoyance popped a post in my head that I texted over for them to contemplate. Someone else recently had me brainstorm topics for their practice and I rattled off songs, an analogy to planting seeds, and then, in contrast, a really academic post. I never give these ideas for any other reason than it's fun to brainstorm content that might help someone else. (And if it's not something they're interested in, I don't intrude—because part of generosity is knowing when it's not welcome or you've gone over the top.)

You get the point. It can be a good idea to help others and a great idea for building better professional relationships. It's also important that you practice receiving support from others. It shifts the work from being one-sided to having a mutually supportive component that makes the relationship not just stronger (and more likely to keep you in mind) but quite frankly, healthier.

The Complexity of Generosity

In a professional world that often feels innately competitive—be the first to get the work, get the biggest piece, hold the big idea close—being generous feels like a nice virtue that constantly competes with the business model and career goals at hand. But what if this idea of radical generosity is the key to creating a self-sustaining practice?

Let's consider how they might influence your practice on all levels:

- **Talking to the worried client** is a small act of generosity. You aren't trying to solve the problem (unless they are asking you to), you're simply present and focused on them. This makes the client feel appreciative of the support.

- **Sharing credit and investing time in training your team** is a bigger act that is often noticed and appreciated. This shares success with others.

- **Introducing a colleague to a client.** This actively creates opportunity for others and eases the way for others to build their own network, not to mention possibly bringing in more work for all of you.

- **Inviting colleagues and clients together for a meal.** This has the exponential impact of good people knowing good people.

Then you start to worry: *the client is taking advantage of your time; the team will try to take your credits and leave you struggling to hit your numbers; the colleague will try to take the client or encroach on your relationship; you won't be invited to the next meal.*

The worry muscle is incredibly strong; it often overpowers the intent of generosity and leaves you doing nothing rather than trusting that the ripple effect of kindness will not only shine through but serve as a powerful energy to build a stronger, healthier practice.

What feeds the worry muscle? Scarcity. It tells you that there is simply not enough work to go around. You need to race to the good work and grab what you can to make sure it's yours. Each of these "races" creates an environment that shuts off creativity, connection, and collaboration.

What you are left with is a decision on how you want to practice and whether you are content to rely on the worry muscle or are willing to build the muscle of generosity, giving it a fighting chance against the very loud suggestions that you have to keep chasing and racing to rise to the top.

While it would be nice to just shout, "I no longer believe in scarcity!" or "I am all about abundance!" the implementation of putting it into practice takes a bit more. But before you are going to start generously showing up for colleagues and clients with your ideas and time, you need to believe that you aren't getting elbowed out at every turn.

You know the scene: a new project comes in and you hear the murmurings about it around the hallways. Suddenly, that partner has a popular office. Everyone is hanging around, wanting to get in on it. Knowing not everyone can get a piece, the vultures are circling. Just like trying to get that last piece of pie at the summer barbecue. Lurking takes on an art form. As it turns out, this is a terrible strategy when it comes to building a practice. Instead of trying to grab your piece of pie, what if you could just create more pie?

Build a Pie Factory

What in the world does this mean? It means instead of racing for one piece of work (that may or may not be worth it once you've got it), start looking to build exponential opportunities. When you flip your mindset to that of building work, your power and control suddenly are guiding your practice rather than reacting to the worry muscle.

The self-sustaining practice is one that knows how to make more opportunity. From there you can take a deep breath and add meaningful value to clients and work upfront rather than making sure it's yours before engaging in any conversation. This shift in viewpoint will allow you to:

- Show up for others.

- Be expansive in your thinking and approach.

- Recognize that relationships are two-sided (accepting generosity is as important as giving).

At the crux of *Might I Suggest* is a generous spirit that you are giving ideas and energy to the clients and thinking expansively about the options you have to help them out. Specific acts of generosity open the door for much bigger business than forcing yourself to try and capitalize on every six minutes you invest in your practice.

As it turns out, most of the strategies in this book have generosity as the core value that invests in clients and extends the business from being transactional to a more meaningful relationship that lasts longer than any one project, case, or deal. Consider how each of these has generosity as its core value:

1. **Linger for a longer conversation** with the client who wants to catch up. Just pausing symbolizes your openness to investing yourself in the relationship.

2. **Send an article** that a client might find interesting. Again, not solely for the purpose of being given work but for helping them out.

3. **Introduce two people** that you think could benefit from knowing each other, with no strings attached or expected benefits for you. Just a mutual connection to help build their networks or solve a problem for them both.

PRACTICE RADICAL GENEROSITY

4. **Offer up connections** whenever you see them in different facets of your network.

5. **Sit down and talk. All the time.** Simply allow the conversations to unfold, be mutually supportive, and allow yourself to be present. Your presence is the opportunity opener.

When you deconstruct a book of business and how it evolved, it is often a story of catching up with someone—being engaged in a conversation—that led to ideas that led to engagements. Show up for that. Not just in hopes of work, but because you care. That single choice radiates through your actions and interactions and how you will feel about your days (and practice).

Radical generosity is the culmination of the entire process of showing up for this new practice and way of thinking about your book of business. Owning your practice allows you to pick the values and embody them into all you do for yourself and clients to cultivate the work and show up in your representation of them. It also asks you to think bigger and notice when the worry muscle is taking over your choices or influencing the way you talk about work or try to build your practice.

Case Study: Excellence Is an Awesome Client Generator

Meet my client, Meredith. She is a big law partner with a thriving practice. More impressive than her practice is her extensive network and the way radical generosity works within that network. My work with Meredith was focused on cultivating a steadiness in her book that didn't just allow her to rise into the higher ranks of firm partnership, but make sure she wasn't left worrying about it year after year.

Leaning into Meredith's strengths, we focused on consistent connections and a steady approach to knowing clients, her colleagues and friends, and showing up to simply be present. Meredith is strong and capable but also knows how to let her expertise speak for itself. She is diligent in reporting to herself (and me) the successes of her week, outstanding questions, and open ideas. She follows up, but most of all she cares.

This care for clients and colleagues isn't rushed or formulaic. It exudes from everything she does and is simply who she is as a human being. She generously connects others and speaks honestly about her personal path and goals. She invites others into her home and is invested in the goals and ideas of her clients and community.

This kind of steadiness doesn't just cultivate good results; it attracts incredible humans who want to work with Meredith. This win-win isn't about being someone else but allowing others to know exactly the excellence they get when working with and knowing Meredith.

***

The concept of plenty shifts you from chasing work to attracting exponential amounts of aligned work that allows your expertise to shine and evolve. Bringing abundance and generosity together creates radical results. Radical generosity assumes that there is more than enough to go around.

Your Task List

1. **As CEO of your book of business, practice cultivating practical generosity as a core value.** Pick three interesting and helpful resources you can share with clients. It might be a set of articles, a checklist, your latest client alert, or a couple questions that every client seems to ask.

2. **Pick two people within your network who need to know each other.** Make an introduction and allow others to benefit from knowing each other. Step out of the way to allow them space for a new relationship.

3. **Practice generosity.** Start by engaging in conversations with your team (and clients) that are focused on knowing more about them and their goals. What are they wanting to experience or lead the charge on next? What clients would they like to be working with or how do they describe their own ideal clients? Pick one way you can help move their goals forward and take the time to follow through on this investment in others.

In Conclusion: Believe in Exponential Results

After my wake-up call in 2019, I made a commitment to change how I work and live. More importantly, I made a commitment to share my solutions and process, so it wouldn't just benefit me, but you, as well. As a community and profession, building a thriving book of business with clients that keep coming back for more has to work with life happening, not solely when it's calm. Whether you like it or not, life is rarely calm for long.

Before I send you off with a charge to go out and own your practice as the CEO you are meant to be, I need to share a bit about what happens at this stage. Throughout the pages of this book, I have shared the strategies that allow you to shift the view of your practice from hoping it works to cultivating a self-sustaining book of business that shifts not only how clients see you, but how you see yourself. But now that you've reached the end of this book, it's up to you to focus on the heart of what you do and why you do it. It is a choice to become this professional.

My wish for you is to go out and shine. Find a light within you for the life you want to live. Find the practice, team, and clients that spark that inner student in you who loves a good challenge or a great brainstorming session. Be true to who you are and what you're looking for in a practice. It's simply the easiest way to build a book; without it, the results are impossible to gauge. Finally, have patience with yourself and your practice. A good deep breath goes a long way in figuring out the next best step.

Remember: A self-sustaining practice isn't selfish—it is smart.

The world is filled with the noise of marketers and social media thriving off messaging meant to make you feel small, in search of the "one solution," and constantly wanting more that's top of mind, yet out of reach. I'm here to tell you that more is right in front of you for the taking. You don't need big blocks of time or to try and do everything.

Find your joy and what interests and excites you in the world. It helps you see the path ahead with better vision and a clear lens. Know that bad days and bumps happen because you are growing—not to limit your growth.

Start with little bites and the easiest options to build momentum and start measuring your results.

One more strategy nudge: Pick just two things each week to focus on that support you and your practice, and in turn, your colleagues, clients, and community.

Step up and introduce yourself, talk to your clients and colleagues, and share your work. Make two choices each week that are aligned and deliberate choices for you and the practice you want to grow.

Why two? Two is doable. And when you have two connections and conversations a week for fifty-two weeks, that's

104 meaningful moments in a year. This is not just significant, but impressive.

This will allow you to make new relationships and invest in those that are already part of your network. It will allow you to find a way to share your work that is aligned with your clients and their goals. It will allow you to find a rhythm that can be ramped up or down as time and client goals necessitate.

As the final entry on that monthly meeting of yours, tell me about your connections and conversations this month. And if you want to take it up a notch, let's work through this together as we put together your master list of 104 Meaningful Connections and Conversations.

Until next time ... Deb

Acknowledgments

I must start with my family. Starting with your light-ning-speed response to that 4 a.m. email, to every phone call I twisted and turned into a book chapter brainstorm, I appreciate you and all you have done to support me and my work. To my kids, Andrew (and even the dogs)—your willingness to hunker down and think through a book with me makes my work not really work and the writing a part of who I get to be with you.

A big shout out and thank you to my book banterers (and critiquers): Ryan Hopkins: you listened when this book was just an idea that blended the amazing results that happen with consistent focus not just in the gym but with our clients and conversations. Gianni, Jules, and Michael: your willing-ness to fight with me over content and make strong requests for the sake of a better book is beyond appreciated. And to Anne, who not only introduced me to needlepointing but was willing to take a sharp pen to the content when I just couldn't any longer.

Finally, I say it all the time: I have the very best clients out there. Each of you continue to confirm my belief that client relationships are the crux of a strong business. For those that answered those emails in 2019, you exemplify the meaning of a mutually supportive relationship. To all who joined in Lab sessions where exercises were tested and feedback given (over and over again), you are an essential part of this book and my practice. For those who generously shared their stories within these pages, thank you for allowing others to get a glimpse of you and your story. Getting to be a part of your work stories and world is an honor, each and every day. The cartwheels, happy dances, and confetti moments are pure joy.

To my writing team: A huge thanks to Amy Barton for the incredible editing, and to Scott MacMillan and the Grammar Factory team for your hard work, willingness to debate about punctuation, and taking my crazy calls from my very first idea (which often starts before the last book ends). To the Smith Publicity team, you continue to be the gold standard of excellence, and I am honored to have you helping me share my work with the world. Each of you inspire me to continue sharing the stories and practical guides that come next.

About the Author

Deb Feder is a business development and client relationship coach and strategist focused on helping lawyers and professionals bring in consistent clients through curious, confident conversations and interesting content. Deb's programs offer simple and effective strategies to build, manage, and grow meaningful relationships with colleagues, clients, and industry partners. Prior to founding Feder Development, Deb practiced corporate law for fifteen years; she holds a history degree from the University of Michigan and her JD/MBA from the University of Iowa.

Deb is the author of *Tell Me More: Building Trusted Client Relationships through Everyday Interactions* and *After Hello: How to Build a Book of Business, One Conversation at a Time*, additional practical guides to the mindset, strategy, and conversations necessary to cultivate a career you love with a thriving book of business. Deb's work has been featured in Fast Company, Bloomberg Law, Law360, and many industry podcasts. Deb is a slow runner, avid traveler and cook, and beginner at needlepoint. Deb lives in Kansas City with her family and two disobedient dogs.